Doing It Right:

The Fundamentals of Better Diving

Jarrod Jablonski

Doing It Right: The Fundamentals of Better Diving

Printed in Canada

ISBN 0-9713267-0-3

Front Cover: (Top) Two divers set off to explore the deep reefs of Bimini, Bahamas. Photo by Dickie Walls. (Lower left) Wreck diving in Fernando de Noronha, Brazil. Photo by Pedro Paulo Cunha. (Lower Right) DIR's clean gear configuration. Photo by Steve Auer

Back Cover: (Top) Bimini's coral wall, from 275 feet down. Photo by Dickie Walls. (Center) WKPP survey team heads off into a Mexican cenote. Photo by Steve Auer. (Bottom) Jarrod Jablonski gets ready for a dive with the Halcyon RB80 Rebreather at Wakulla Springs State Park. Photo by David Rhea

DIR gear configuration photos for Chapter 6 by Steve Auer, www.aquatograph.com

Doing It Right:
The Fundamentals of Better Diving

Jarrod Jablonski

Global Underwater Explorers
High Springs

Acknowledgements

This manual represents a collective effort, one motivated by the desire to share a love of the aquatic realm with others. So many great people from GUE members and friends to associates and volunteers make these things possible that for every name represented below there are at least ten behind the scenes. I am grateful to all the many people that support GUE and to Dr. Eddie Brian, Dr. Panos Alexakos, Dr. Todd Kincaid, and Mark Lonsdale for their advice, writing skills, and knowledge. For their diligence in assembling this manual a special thanks to Anthony Rue, Myrna Coubrough, Nanci LeVake, Dawn Kernagis, Harry Averill and to all the talented photographers whose pictures grace this book. I am also grateful to Rebecca Fry, Michael Kane, and the entire GUE instructor contingent for their tireless support, dedication, and encouragement. Thanks also to George Irvine, Casey McKinlay, Jess Armantrout, Scott Landon, and all the members of the Woodville Karst Plain Project for their support and assistance. Lasting appreciation also goes to the thousands of international GUE supporters that provide the infrastructure for these very accomplishments. Lastly, and most importantly, thanks to my family without whose love and dedication none of this would have been possible.

Contents

©Sandra Edwards, Ft. Lauderdale

From recreational open water diving to deep ocean and cave, the "Doing it Right" approach enhances all types of diving.

Preface

Why This Book

This book was written for anyone who wants to get the most out of their diving. It makes no difference if you are interested only in augmenting safety, or in raising the enjoyment quotient of your family's Caribbean diving trip, or in deep cave exploration. This text was written with every diver in mind, regardless of environment or focus, who is interested in improving his/her diving skills. Towards that end, it outlines not only the essential skills and techniques constituting sound diving practice—an analysis of which has been noticeably absent from the repertoires of most dive educators—but also the central elements of a holistic approach to diving. Of course, the most robust equipment configuration available to today's diver is central to the Doing It Right approach.

Note, however, that this book was not designed to teach uncertified individuals how to dive. While new or uncertified divers are encouraged to read this book as a prelude to their own training, this book was not designed as a substitute to proper instruction; its intended audience is certified divers with a basic understanding of SCUBA diving. Furthermore, all references to advanced diving techniques—e.g., mixed gas diving, cave diving, wreck diving, and deep diving—are meant simply as introductory remarks to very specialized activities; they are not intended to stand alone. Technical divers may find that these remarks are geared to less experienced divers; nonetheless, thinking through these "introductory" remarks will certainly benefit even the most experienced diver.

The book itself follows a logical progression. It begins with a thorough treatment of those basic skills that are essential for any good diver to have, and culminates with a discussion of accident analysis and its value for the recreational diver. The book addresses a whole host of issues, ranging from the philosophical underpinnings of DIR, to equipment concerns, to surveys of more advanced forms of diving/training. Although it would be best to read the chapters in the sequence they appear, most chapters are self-contained. So, if one cannot bear the suspense, they can go directly to their specific area of interest. Everyone will be well served to read the text start to finish. Even highly experienced technical divers, who may be drawn primarily to equipment issues, will find themselves clearer on the details after giving some thought to a discussion of basic skills. In the end, every element broached here plays an instrumental role in the formation of a sound diver, one whose skill, knowledge, judgment, fitness, and insight into the logic of sound configuration, enables him/her to meet the demands posed by the environments s/he selects to dive in.

One of the forces driving GUE is the desire to forge exactly that kind of diver. GUE is a broad-based, non-profit organization with a wide range of international research and exploration initiatives, promoting DIR as a means to maximize diving fun. DIR is a philosophical approach to scuba diving, holistic in conception, which elaborates the essential elements of sound diving practice. Generally speaking, DIR (Doing it Right) is a system of diving that blends sound diving practices with the world's most refined equipment configuration. Internationally renown for its success, simplicity, and safety, DIR is a diving philosophy that promotes rational choices with respect to dive teams, dive preparation, and equipment configuration as a means of ensuring safety, efficiency, and enjoyment. From deep and overhead diving to recreational reef dives DIR is revolutionizing diving, making it safer and more enjoyable for everyone who chooses to embrace it. By writing this text, GUE wants to share this system with the public and thereby promote in-water safety, efficiency and enjoyment.

We hope that you enjoy this text, that it enriches your diving as it did ours, and that you continue to explore the far reaches of the underwater world in the safest, most efficient way possible.

Safe diving,

JJ

©Ron De Amorim, Ft. Lauderdale

Though good training is necessary to produce a solid base of experience, no amount of training can replace time in the water for honing your skills and for developing comfort, confidence and awareness.

Chapter 1

What Am I Missing?

Diving can be one of life's most unique and enjoyable activities. Few environments are as majestic or intriguing as those we encounter underwater. Floating weightless, one is often filled with excitement and confronted by rare beauty. Each diving location offers divers potentially new experiences and new sights and sounds, ones ranging from historical artifacts to beautiful aquatic life; the underwater world is unparalleled in the rewards it offers a diver.

Regardless of whether one is a deep wreck diver, cave diver, shallow ocean diver or lake diver, all recreational (non-paid) divers share a common motive for diving; namely, they want to have fun. Typically, people take up diving for recreational reasons. This, in turn, has resulted in an industry that has emphasized short and easy training over proficiency, and in divers who have been led to believe that recreational diving requires little if any dedication to skill mastery or physical fitness.

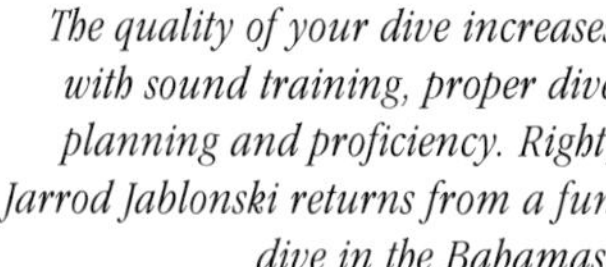

The quality of your dive increases with sound training, proper dive planning and proficiency. Right, Jarrod Jablonski returns from a fun dive in the Bahamas.

©David Rhea, Bimini

This is a mistake. SCUBA diving is like any other active sport in that one's ability to enjoy it is closely linked to whether one has mastered the fundamental skills of their sport and to whether one is comfortable performing these. Regardless of whether one is skiing, bicycling, hiking, or climbing, people who are reasonably fit and who are proficient in the skill set of their sport simply have more fun. This is not to say that one must be gifted to enjoy an activity, only that the more proficient in an activity one is, the more fun one will have performing that activity.

Improperly developed diving skills, poor technique, and inefficient equipment often result in unnecessary exertion and more stress, and thus in less fun. Recognizing this, divers around the world have come to promote increased diving proficiency as the necessary means of satisfying their desire for enjoyment underwater. From improved safety to more fun and enjoyment, divers are realizing that "streamlined" diving courses and lax training are not serving their best interests, and that better preparedness in diving is necessary in order to reach their goals. This movement towards better preparedness is at the heart of a very popular diving style called Doing it Right, or simply DIR. Initiated by diving enthusiasts like you, DIR proposes a simple and robust diving style that enables divers to have more fun with less stress and greater safety.

The beauty of DIR lies in its simple design, its logical evolution, and its unparalleled flexibility. Regardless of whether one is a recreational reef diver, a world record cave diver, or a deep wreck explorer, the tenets of DIR are identical. Without question the most popular and effective diving system ever devised, DIR involves creating a solid foundation of diving skills and supporting these with the world's most robust equipment configuration.

Divers, however, are usually led to believe that different diving environments require radically different equipment and techniques. If this is the case, how can DIR be a system for all divers?

©Achim Schlöffel, Croatia

The DIR equipment configuration is easily transferred from open water to all forms of technical diving.

The Real Story

The diving community has led (and continues to lead) people to believe that there is a **radical** difference between the procedures and equipment a diver would use within the limits of standard recreational diving and those s/he would use outside these. The "truths" that support this position are intimately linked to both a distrust of unconventional (i.e., deep or technical) diving and to a desire to make diving more "accessible" to the diving public. Making diving more "accessible" is generally synonymous with making it easier, in allowing educators to shorten diver training.

Some environments require very special training, but all environments demand sound training principles. Right, divers enjoy an afternoon dive in a Florida cave.

©Steve Auer

Together, reduced training time, relaxed skill requirements, and an entirely casual atmosphere produce a picture of diving that sells it as a skill requiring little investment in time or energy. This perception, in turn, is supported by a set of "streamlined" courses that seek profitability by emphasizing brevity and future diver training. In truth, this view of diving often leads to unqualified individuals pursuing activities well beyond their level of comfort, and in more stress and less diving fun.

It is not difficult to convince new open water divers that deep divers are either crazy or that their equipment configuration is (and must be) essentially different from their own. What is difficult is making them see that, in actuality, the techniques of sound deep diving are not *fundamentally* different from those they *should* be using in recreational open water diving. This is not to say, however, that open water divers are capable of advanced or technical diving; these activities do, in fact, require substantially greater refinement, often with specialized skills and equipment. What it does say is that regardless of what kind of diving one does, proper skill development is the key to the successful pursuit of all.

Properly trained divers should possess a fundamental set of skills. This is not the case with many of today's certified divers. Because many educators today are focusing on reducing the training time required to "qualify" open water divers, there is little time left for them to cultivate diving proficiency. In fact, many open water training programs have been reduced from an already short period (an insufficient four days) to an even shorter one (a "subjective" training period). These changes are resulting in the open water community becoming progressively less prepared to take on the challenges of underwater exploration. It is also becoming progressively more alienated from the domain of the skilled technical diver. This usually entails that the average open water diver will be incapable of even recognizing what in the capable technical diver would be an important skill set for him/her to have. This is a dangerous combination. Divers with weak open water skills are not only unprepared to confront the demands of the aquatic realm, they are even less prepared to pursue more ambitious diving, should the desire surface to pursue it. In short, these divers are neither safe nor efficient; they rarely get the most out of their diving.

What Makes a Good Diver?

Though it is true that equipment and procedures used for different environments *can* be very different, the fundamental components of sound diving practice do not necessarily change much with different environments. Essential to all environments, there are three fundamental components to good diving, namely: *diving experience, diving ability, and a robust equipment configuration.* Of these three, diving experience is the one most relevant to a particular diving environment; obviously an inexperienced open water diver will likely not fair well on a deep wreck dive.

Diving Experience

Experience is key to becoming a good diver; it is the result of training and of familiarity with the demands posed by the varying environments in which one dives. Therefore, diver training is the first step to safely gain useful individual experience. As an individual becomes more experienced, they necessarily become more skilled.

Divers who learn their fundamental skills from a professional educator are in a much better position to gain experience safely and effectively. New diving environments are often replete with unseen dangers, and untrained persons who venture there place themselves at great risk. For example, untrained divers who try to penetrate a wreck or a cave, who venture below ice or who try to explore the deep, are often oblivious to the fundamental safety considerations that are attached to these ventures. Tragically, by being unaware of these, they end up violating them, and many die. Robust diver instruction can provide individuals with the vital information and training that will allow them to safely explore new environments and build experience.

Though good training is necessary to producing a solid base of experience, no amount of training can replace time in the water for honing one's skills and for developing comfort, confidence and awareness. In other words, familiarity and comfort with what a given diving task demands require repeated exposure to those demands. Once a diver develops, through the right diver training programs, a solid foundation of diving skills, s/he should then pursue an active diving regimen that will progressively build upon these skills. By committing themselves to the water, by refining their techniques and by progressively expanding the type of dives they can comfortably undertake, these divers will slowly expand their experience.

Too many divers and diving educators undervalue the process of gaining experience outside course training. Dive training is essential in the process of creating a good foundation, but only diving experience can build the skills and awareness that create a good diver.

Diving Ability

Diving ability involves knowledge, natural aptitude, and practised technique. Though knowledge and technique are well within the control of a motivated diver, natural aptitude is not. Some divers are naturally more gifted; they are intrinsically more skillful and more comfortable in the water than others. Nonetheless, individuals who are not intrinsically gifted in the water can often compensate for this lack of natural ability by becoming more knowledgeable and by working on their technique. Practice dramatically improves diving ability and many divers who initially struggled in the water eventually became exceptional divers by remaining dedicated to becoming more knowledgeable and to augmenting their skills.

Ideally, divers would become knowledgeable and develop good

technique while undergoing course training. However, this is unrealistic; most training requires that divers undergo additional skill training and literature review. When coupled with a good physical fitness program, these training supplements substantially promote diver improvement.

There are many supplementary course materials that enable divers to become more knowledgeable. These can be found listed in the resources section of the present manual and include: sources for online discussion lists, resource locations, and information regarding GUE membership. GUE membership is a unique way of becoming more knowledgeable about diving in that membership entitles one not only to active discussion lists on a host of diving related issues, but also to a quarterly magazine that caters specifically to divers seeking to improve their diving skills and to expand their knowledge.

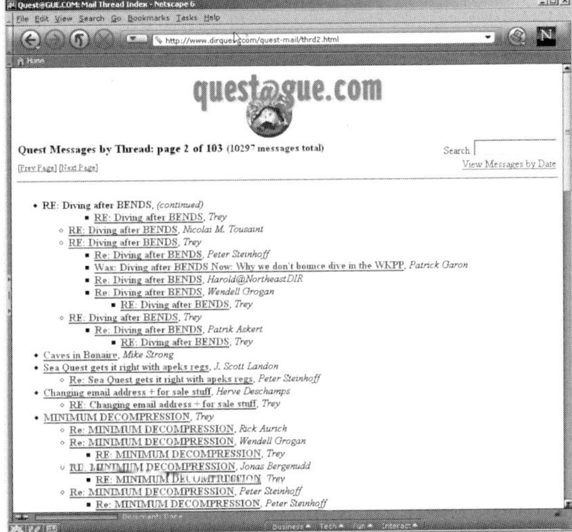

Online resources, like the GUE mailing list Quest and the website dirquest.com, help to extend your knowledge of DIR diving beyond the classroom.

The Purpose of this Book: Having Fun

Ultimately, the purpose of this book is to help you have more fun. As a means to this, this book will: 1) help you identify and correct potential deficiencies in your diving; 2) outline the world's most successful diving system- Doing it Right (DIR). From diving proficiency and dive planning, to optimal breathing mixes and basic rescue, this material will radically help you be safer and have more fun; and 3) provide you with a sound system for engaging in future diver training. This will range from ways to pick a good educator, to how to pursue personal study and expand your knowledge. This, in turn, will open you up to entirely new areas of diving, increase your personal safety and reduce your stress while diving. In short, this book will show you how to have more fun.

The DIR demo provides valuable hands-on learning.

DIR education opens up new underwater vistas to the diver.

CHAPTER 2

LEARNING HOW TO LEARN

Choosing among the array of promises made by agencies and the individuals that represent them can seem like a daunting challenge. Their claims to be the "best" or of the highest "quality" seem to blend together, often leaving the prospective student-diver with a difficult choice to make. Yet, choosing a qualified instructor can be one of the most important choices of one's diving career. Certainly, many individuals have overcome sloppy instruction and become excellent divers; but a good instructor, by providing a solid foundation upon which divers can progress safely while building advanced diving skills, greatly facilitates the learning and proficiency process.

WHY IS IT SO HARD TO FIND A GOOD DIVING EDUCATOR?

Unfortunately, most dive shops striving to compete in today's crowded diving market offer heavily devalued or "discounted" dive education. This is because they have been led to believe that in order to promote diving activity and equipment sales, they must discount their training. Therefore, most dive courses are pitifully inexpensive, leaving little incentive for qualified educators to offer them. At first glance, increased competition and reduced prices seem to favor consumers. However, on closer examination, it is unlikely that many qualified educators will be willing to work for what often amounts to hourly wages that fall well below the national minimum wage. The average dive consumer ends up buying a pale image of what s/he could have purchased. Given that one's safety is at stake here, it is questionable, then, whether ultimately these discounted prices promote the interests of the average dive consumer.

In their hopeless quest to gain and maintain their own advantage through competitive pricing, most shops in a given area charge similar rates; as a result, few divers are actually aware of this abysmal pay scale. Even divers for whom cost is nearly irrelevant are left paying substandard wages to often less-than-qualified instructors. Actually, even individuals on the tightest of budgets could afford the additional costs that would attract a qualified educator. In other words, if one can afford to dive, then one can't afford not to learn properly.

Low wages mean that many diving instructors often fall into two categories. They are either inexperienced individuals who are not able to earn better wages elsewhere, or they are extremely dedicated divers who love the activity enough to live far below the poverty line. Unfortunately, the latter is not common enough. Yet, some instructors are resisting the "less for less" trend and are charging a fair wage for quality instruction. Of course, high rates do not necessarily make a good instructor, but they do increase one's chances of hiring a professional educator.

Since good educators are difficult to find, this often means that people will have to travel to find quality diver training.The question, then, is how does one evaluate an instructor, especially if they must do it long distance?

Author preparing for deep wall research dive. Good instructors must maintain personal diving skills with non-class related experience.

©David Rhea, Bimini

What is the instructor's personal diving history?

Unfortunately, there seems to be a growing number of instructors that lack personal experience in what they are offering to teach. It is all too common for instructors to claim dozens or hundreds of dives as proof of experience. However, these dives (if true) are often teaching dives and not personally demanding. In choosing an instructor, be sure that the instructor does the kind of diving for which one is considering training, and that s/he does so on his/her own time; doing so will give one access to a great deal of useful information. Before deciding, ask the instructor for a resume, and ask those locally what their experience has been with the prospective educator. Individuals can often get a sense of an instructor by personally discussing course content and structure.

How Often does the Instructor Teach and/or Dive?

There are some very good instructors who teach casually (i.e., they hold conventional jobs in addition to teaching). However, when evaluating whether such an instructor is the right choice, try to establish how much time s/he spends in the water. While instructors with regular jobs may seem preferable in that they are less caught up in the business of the certification process, and more inclined to focus on quality instruction, their normal job, coupled with their teaching and a daily fitness routine, may leave them little time for the personal dives that will make them an optimal choice. Instructors that do not dive recreationally are not taxing their own abilities and are not accumulating the experience that will allow them to relay valuable information. Find out how often a diving instructor is in the water and ask about the diving s/he does outside of teaching. Also find out how much additional training the instructor has undertaken; e.g., do they teach open water specialties beyond basic certification? Have they pursued more advanced forms of technical diving?

Does your prospective instructor participate in recreational diving in demanding environments?

©Pedro Paulo Cunha, Fernando de Noronha, Brazil

Instructors that do not make an effort to remain current with developments in their field or that do not maintain a reasonable level of fitness are unlikely to make very efficient educators. Maintaining a quality educational presence is about much more than an original investment. Instead, it involves a great deal of dedication, with regular fitness training, personal diving, and academic review.

Educate Yourself

The tricky salesman might say that there are few things more frustrating than an educated consumer. Being knowledgeable will not only allow a student to evaluate a prospective instructor's competencies, it will also allow them to identify inconsistencies between what one knows to be true and what the instructor might propose; this knowledge, in turn, will put the student in a good position to ask for an explanation and evaluate the response.

Beyond the instructor issue, all student-divers will benefit from a prolonged period of pre-course study. Divers that consider pursuing advanced or technical diver training should review course materials and discuss the course structure and material with their prospective instructor. This will assist them in developing a better sense of his/her ability and professionalism.

Don't be Fooled by the Discount Structure

Nearly everyone understands that in the grand scheme of things we get what we pay for. However, rarely does recognition of this truth keep people from trying to get more for less. Educators that play pricing games or offer discount training either simply do not value their own time or offer less for the money. It is ironic that people will spend thousands of dollars on equipment and travel, but struggle to save a couple hundred dollars on an education that could save their lives.

The Agency

Should an instructor's agency affiliation make any difference in the selection process? The most common recommendation for finding a qualified educator is to ask friends and associates. While this is typically sound advice, it leaves open the question of the relative merits of the different agencies to which instructors belong. After all, is not the main thrust of different organizations better training? That they offer better training? Why, then, would most people contend that, in choosing an instructor, one should ignore what agency they certify under? Because, traditionally: 1) most training was fairly similar, 2) the requirements barely distinguishable, and 3) most active instructors taught for a host of different organizations simply to avail themselves of different student preferences. As these are less evident today, when evaluating whether to engage a given instructor, it would be wise for a prospective student-diver to look into what agency the instructor under consideration represents. The relevant questions one should ask of an agency are not unlike those asked of an instructor. For example, what level of experience does it demand of a diver seeking a particular class? What steps does it take to ensure diving safety, experience, currency, fitness, and professionalism in their educators?

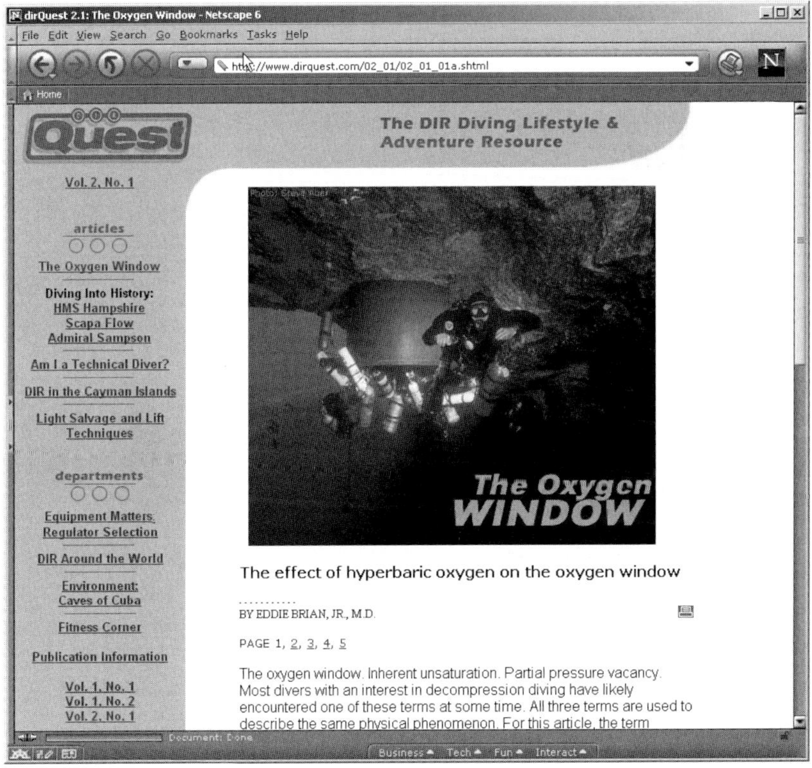

The Global Underwater Explorers websites, www.gue.com, www.dirquest.com, and www.doingitright.org, bring together instructors, new and experienced divers, and dive researchers in a unique community focused on improving the quality of diver education.

©Pedro Paulo Cunha, Fernando de Noronha, Brazil

A solid foundation is essential preparation for all levels of diving.

Chapter 3

Building a Solid Foundation

Skilled divers possess an array of talents and abilities; some of these are specific to the particular environment they dive (e.g., good reel work), some are not (e.g., good buoyancy). Nonetheless, as most fundamental skills will serve them wherever they choose to dive, divers should strive to be capable in all environments.

Basic Diving Skills

Historically, the degree of aquatic skill necessary to become an open water diver has been the subject of a great deal of debate. Unfortunately, most organizations seem more intent on reducing training time than in improving diving ability. Though, as with any new activity, it is reasonable to expect that the skills of new divers will not be refined, and that they will struggle with these. Nonetheless there are certain skills and a certain level of conditioning that we can expect from any diver.

Today, there are dozens of diving agencies, offering many more different certification courses, in skill-sets ranging from basic open water to advanced Trimix instructor. Though divers emerging from these courses often possess vastly different skill and experience levels, nonetheless, the fact is that most seem to lack sound fundamental diving skills. From instructors to open water divers, these divers are often found unskilled in important areas like good buddy awareness, efficient diver propulsion, and good buoyancy control. In fact, lack of skill in these areas consistently results in unnecessary stress, fatigue, and even fatalities. Poor diving technique can greatly increase diver stress and reduce individual ability to manage emergency situations. Most emergency situations result from a cumulative effect, often involving poor diving technique and/or awareness. For example, divers with good buoyancy and trim are

Basic skills such as buoyancy control and efficient propulsion are a must when diving in a potentially silty environment.

©Ron De Amorim

far less prone to unnecessary stress and much better prepared to manage diving problems.

Before beginning our treatment of those basic skills we contend to be at the foundation of all good diving practice, it is important to note the following. It is natural that, on the whole, advanced divers will be more skilled than novice divers, and that we can expect more from the former than we can from the latter; that is only reasonable. Advanced divers are often in more demanding environments than novice divers, environments that demand greater skill and awareness. Cave or wreck divers, for example, unlike open water divers, routinely must contend with an overhead, with silt, current and complexities of navigation; the environment they dive in mandates that they are more skilled. What this means for our present discussion is that when evaluating whether a given diver has sound basic diving skills, it is important to match their own skill-set with the environment in which they are being used. In other words, the skill level considered acceptable for a novice open water diver is not acceptable, in fact it is potentially deadly, for a cave or wreck diver. Passable or even exceptional skills in one environment may be marginal or insufficient in another.

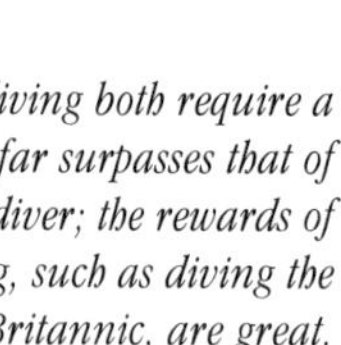

Wreck and cave diving both require a skill level which far surpasses that of the novice diver; the rewards of advanced training, such as diving the HMS Britannic, are great.

©Jarrod Jablonski

So, what basic skills form the foundation of sound diving practice? In addition to being comfortable in the water and reasonably fit—a necessary condition for athletic competence in general—a good diver's skill-set should include: buoyancy control, mask clearing, gas management, propulsion techniques, trim control, equipment management, directional and buddy awareness.

Aquatic Comfort

General fitness is an essential part of becoming a healthy individual and a good diver. However, individuals can be in excellent physical condition and not be comfortable in the water. Divers who are very fit, but not particularly comfortable swimming, should invest some training time in increasing their swimming proficiency. Several lessons with a good swimming coach will immediately make a huge difference in an individual's swimming ability. Good swimming technique can easily triple one's distance while reducing swim times and effort. Good swimming ability, while increasing comfort, proficiency, and safety, will make a diver better and his/her diving more fun.

Though not technically a skill, fitness is a necessary prerequisite of any skill and the basis of sound diving in general. Fit individuals are more comfortable encountering physical stress and are more likely to effectively manage strenuous situations. By extension, fit divers are more capable of handling the stresses of daily diving and therefore able to have more fun. Furthermore, improved fitness reduces the risk of panic, increases the types of environments that divers can explore, reduces the risk of diving related injuries, enables divers to help their team members, and improves diver safety.

Note: Review the section on physical fitness in this manual for more information on how fitness impacts one's diving proficiency and personal health. Furthermore, consult www.gue.com for more detailed information on fitness routines for divers.

Yasemin Dalkilic's mastery of freediving skills has shattered world records for breath-hold diving.

©Gido Brasse, Bodrum, Turkey

There are a number of ways to measure individual fitness. Obviously, individuals who focus on one form of exercise at the exclusion of other forms will be more fit than others when performing that exercise. Generally speaking, however, individuals are best served by engaging in a variety of exercises. Nonetheless, in practice, it is what will motivate an individual most that most likely will be the best exercise for that person.

Where Do You Rank in Any or All of the Following Categories?

A. Swimming:

• Minimum Fitness	Swim 400 meters continuously
• Medium Fitness	Swim 1600 meters continuously
• Advanced Fitness	Swim 5000 meters continuously

B. Jogging:

• Minimum Fitness	Run 30 minutes continuously
• Medium Fitness	Run 60 minutes continuously
• Advanced Fitness	Run 26.2 miles (a marathon)

C. Biking:

• Minimum Fitness	Ride 45 minutes continuously
• Medium Fitness	Ride 3 hours continuously
• Advanced Fitness	Ride 100 miles (a century)

D. Jumping Rope:

• Minimum Fitness	Jump 5 minutes continuously
• Medium Fitness	Jump 15 minutes continuously
• Advanced Fitness	Jump 45 minutes continuously

Divers will benefit greatly from a high level of physical fitness.

©Cameron Martz

Mask Clearing

It is not uncommon for individuals who are just learning how to dive to have trouble clearing their mask. However, many certified divers continue to have problems with mask clearing; and that is disturbing. It is essential that divers master this fundamental skill; inability to properly clear one's mask will inevitably lead to stress, and possibly panic, when one's mask is flooded or kicked off. Struggling through discomfort and frustration in the pool when learning to clear one's mask is far better than panicking when one's mask is dislodged while diving. The former may be uncomfortable; the latter is life threatening.

How are Your Mask Clearing Skills?

Depending on one's level of diving, below is listed a set of drills that will enable student-divers to evaluate their proficiency in mask clearing.

A. New Diver

- Be able to comfortably clear a partially flooded mask within five seconds
- Remove and replace the mask while at depth
- While holding a dive buddy's arm be able to slowly ascend to the surface without a mask

B. Advanced Diver

- Be able to remove, replace, and clear a mask in less than 10 seconds
- While holding a dive buddy's arm swim 50'(15m), replace the mask and ascend slowly
- Be able to buddy breathe (sharing one second stage) with the mask removed

C. Advanced Technical Diver (with complete gear and stage bottles)

- While buddy breathing (sharing one second stage) with the mask removed, swim 100' (30m), replace the mask and clear it in less than five seconds
- While following a line with the mask removed and holding one's breath swim 50'(15m), replace the mask and clear in less than five seconds

Low volume masks reduce effort and increase the field of vision. No matter which type of mask one chooses, comfort in mask-clearing skills will prevent stress should one's mask become dislodged.

Buoyancy Control

Buoyancy control is an essential element of diving proficiency; it is also one of the hardest skills for a new diver to master. Without proper buoyancy control divers not only wreak havoc on their surroundings, they also put themselves in harm's way. From the destruction of coral life, to damaged equipment, to injured divers, poor buoyancy control can have a dramatic impact on both conservation and enjoyment. A diver with poor buoyancy control often struggles to overcome his buoyancy problems by additional physical effort. For example, divers that are not neutral in the water must kick with added effort simply to prevent themselves from sinking. This effort "to remain neutral" does not contribute to forward momentum, and is essentially wasted effort.

Few diving skills are so essential, and yet so under emphasized by the diving community, as buoyancy control. In fact, many stressed or panicked divers (some of whom became fatalities) owe their difficulties to poor buoyancy control. Good buoyancy skills can take time to master, but proficiency in this area pays great dividends over the course of one's diving career.

How is Your Buoyancy?

Depending on one's level of diving, below is listed a set of drills that will enable a student-diver to evaluate their proficiency in buoyancy control.

A. New Diver

- Be able to descend slowly to depth, stopping within 10' (3m) of the bottom
- Float for one minute in a horizontal position while remaining within five feet (1.5m) of the starting depth
- While diving, stop several times and hover horizontally without moving and without adding/subtracting air to/from the Buoyancy Compensator (BCD)

Good buoyancy skills are essential for protecting fragile environments.

©Jarrod Jablonski

B. Advanced Diver

- Be able to descend slowly to depth, stopping within 5'(1.5m) of the bottom
- Do not use one's hands for any buoyancy control or propulsion (they should remain still at all times)
- Float for two minutes in a slightly head down position while remaining within 2' (60cm) of the starting depth
- While floating horizontally pass the regulator to an out of air diver without changing depth more than 5' (1.5m)

C. Advanced Technical Diver (wearing full equipment and stage bottles)

- Be able to descend slowly to depth, stopping within 1' (30cm) from the bottom
- Do not use one's hands for any buoyancy control or propulsion (they should remain still at all times)
- Float for two minutes in a slightly head down position while remaining within 6" (15cm) of the bottom
- Float for two minutes in a slightly head down position while remaining within 1' (30cm) of the starting depth
- While floating horizontally pass the regulator to an out of air diver without changing depth more than 2' (60cm)

Trim

The words trim and buoyancy have commonly been used synonymously. Though they are related, they are two different elements of efficient diving, each requiring practice to master. Proper trim and buoyancy control greatly reduce swimming effort and gas consumption, making dives longer and easier. In contrast to buoyancy, which concerns being "neutral," trim refers to a diver's "attitude" in the water, the degree to which they are horizontal or vertical. Most divers swim in a foot down position using a flutter kick that gives downward thrust. This increases the surface area of the diver and the energy necessary for forward propulsion, thereby creating drag and wasting energy. It is also crucial to realize that the feet down position will usually lead to the disturbance of sediments and to environmental damage.

Good trim requires that a diver move through the water in streamlined position. Usually this is best accomplished with a slightly head down posture, keeping the feet somewhat elevated and away from the bottom. By swimming in a horizontal position divers are far more streamlined, and therefore experience less drag. Coupled to proper buoyancy control, good trim will drastically reduce the effort required to move through the water, will reduce effort and stress and add to one's enjoyment.

Certain BC designs can actually complicate the problem of proper trim. For example, BC's with restrictive bungies appear to promote gas trapping and increased drag by generating turbulent flow around the diver. Trapped gas pockets can imbalance the diver with unequal pockets of lift. Furthermore, traditional jacket-style buoyancy compensators generally lift the upper portion of the body, making it even more difficult to remain horizontal. Practised divers may be able to overcome this shortcoming; but back-mounted buoyancy compensators facilitate proper trim, improving performance and ease of diving.

Proper trim is also negatively affected by conventional open water weighting systems which position the bulk of a diver's weight around the waist. Technical divers usually avoid this impact with the use of double tanks. However, both recreational and technical divers benefit from properly distributing weighting systems. For example, divers can use a stainless steel back plate and place weight below the plate (such as a v-weight for doubles), or on a single tank with the use of a keel weight or weighted backplate.

The gas-trapping characteristics of some BCs make achieving proper trim more difficult, as well as increasing drag. Right, a poor hose configuration creates an entanglement hazzard and increases water turbulence; ©GUE, Florida

A simple BC with a streamlined design promotes proper trim and reduces the effort of swimming; ©David Rhea, Bimini, Bahamas

Steel tanks can also be used to limit the need for additional weight. However, divers must use care not to overweight themselves. Individuals must evaluate their buoyancy to ensure that they are properly weighted and should be able to hold their position in the water at 10 feet (for safety/decompression purposes) while their tanks are nearly empty. Divers that are not properly weighted could float to the surface should an equipment failure cause a loss of the diver's gas. Alternatively, divers who are over-weighted require more air in their BC, increasing drag and the energy necessary for forward momentum. The stress of struggling against improper weighting can, in and of itself, create enough stress to initiate an emergency.

How is Your Trim?

A. New Diver
- Swim through the water with a slightly head down posture
- Descend, gain neutral buoyancy, and start swimming while remaining horizontal

B. Advanced Diver
- Descend, gain neutral buoyancy, and start swimming while remaining horizontal
- Maintain a horizontal posture while air sharing with dive buddy
- While maintaining horizontal position turn full circles in each direction while using only the legs (no hand movement)
- While floating horizontally turn in any direction and back up slowly while using only the legs (no hand movement)

C. Advanced Technical Diver- in full technical equipment with stages
- Descend, gain neutral buoyancy, and start swimming while remaining horizontal
- Maintain a horizontal posture while air sharing with a dive buddy
- Maintain a horizontal position while turning full circles in each direction and using only the legs (no hand movement)
- While floating horizontally turn in any direction and back up slowly while using only the legs (no hand movement)

Gas Management

Advanced divers frequently refer to the contents of their tanks as "gas," because, instead of air, they are often breathing other mixtures, e.g., Nitrox or Trimix. Regardless of what kind of gas a diver is breathing, s/he must always be fully aware of their remaining supply. Far too many divers have lost their lives because they have run out of gas, which in all but the most extreme cases was a result of irresponsibility. Unfortunately, most divers do not get a second chance to learn from such an error. Precise air management is essential to any form of technical diving, e.g., overhead or deep diving; nonetheless, all divers should be fully cognizant of their tank contents.

How Effectively do You Manage Your Breathing Supply?

A. New Diver
- Always able to return to the boat with the requested minimum supply (usually 500-750psi)
- Never run low on breathing supply and able to monitor dive

buddy's supply

- Able to guesstimate cylinder supply prior to looking at gauge (within 500psi/35bar)

B. ADVANCED DIVER

- Always able to return with desired reserve supply and never run low on breathing supply
- Able to guesstimate cylinder supply prior to looking at gauge (within 300psi/20bar)
- Understand and are able to calculate the 1/3 rule for gas management

C. ADVANCED TECHNICAL DIVER

- Always able to return with desired reserve supply and never run low on breathing supply
- Able to guesstimate when 2/3 of breathing supply is depleted (within 200psi/13bar)
- Familiar with dive buddy breathing supply and able to guesstimate within 200psi/13bar
- Intimately familiar with 1/3 rule for gas management and able to adjust for dissimilar tanks and various conditions while in the water
- Familiar with stage and decompression tank air rules and able to adjust relative to activity

PROPULSION TECHNIQUES

There are a variety of propulsion techniques available to divers. The experienced diver alternates between different types of kicks to reduce muscle cramping and to meet the demands of various diving environments. First, by alternating between kicking styles, s/he allows him/herself to rest certain muscles by bringing others into play. Second, by varying a kicking style, an experienced diver can adjust his propulsion technique to the demands of a particular environment. For example, by switching from a frog kick to a modified flutter, the experienced diver can minimize silting in a low, silty, area.

HOW ARE YOUR PROPULSION TECHNIQUES?

A. NEW DIVER

- Demonstrate an efficient flutter kick
- Demonstrate an efficient frog kick
- Alternate between a flutter kick and a frog kick
- Demonstrate fining control by hovering or swimming without moving hands or arms

B. Advanced Diver

- Demonstrate a range of propulsion intensity using both flutter and frog kicks; be able to alternate between the two styles, for example, able to alternate between a careful flutter and frog kick, one required by silty conditions, and a strong open water kick
- Demonstrate an ability to travel across a silty bottom (within 3' (1m) from the bottom)
- While floating horizontally, turn 90 degrees in each direction using only the legs (no hand movement)

C. Advanced Technical Diver

- Demonstrate a range of propulsion intensity using both flutter and frog kicks; be able to alternate between the two styles
- Demonstrate an ability to travel across an extremely silty bottom while fully configured in technical diving equipment within 1' (30cm) from the bottom
- While hovering horizontally turn 360 degrees in each direction using only the legs (no hand movement)
- While floating horizontally be able to turn in any direction and back up slowly while using only the legs (no hand movement)

Diver demonstrating the flutter kick; ©Ron De Amorim

Types of Propulsion Techniques

Individuals that train in silty or overhead environments have cause to be concerned about reductions in visibility. In the wrong environment, a loss of visibility can substantially impact both individual and team safety. Even so, skilled divers can control the likelihood of reduced visibility; with a proper, feet-up swimming profile and reasonable buoyancy control, a good diver can safely travel in very silty environments with no loss of visibility. While some wreck and cave passages are particularly susceptible to diver movement and to exhaust bubbles, with proper technique, most of these can be left undisturbed. On the other hand, errant fin kicks, erratic hand movements or poor trim can rapidly reduce visibility.

A. Modified Flutter

Recreational open water divers are instructed to use a strong flutter kick, focusing on kicking with straight knees from the hips. When properly executed, this kick produces a great deal of power, but also generates significant downward turbulence. Since the thrust from this kick is directed from the end of the fins toward the floor, the result is that, if used in silty conditions, it will disturb the silt and reduce visibility. In silty conditions, divers can use a *modified flutter,* where the diver bends his or her knees, and kicks from the knee, directing the water upward. While kicking, a diver's torso should be flat with their head down; this forces the fins upward. Like all propulsion techniques, this one can be used with a varying degree of force. In areas with easily disturbed sediments, individuals should move slowly and kick lightly, careful always to force the water upward. In very silty areas, divers propel themselves by kicking carefully only with their ankles.

B. Frog Kick

The frog kick is a particularly effective method of controlling the direction of one's thrust. This kick resembles the kicking action of a swimming breaststroke. Its greatest benefit is that it eliminates the vertical component of a flutter kick. While the modified flutter is generally effective, it maintains a vertical kicking movement and re-

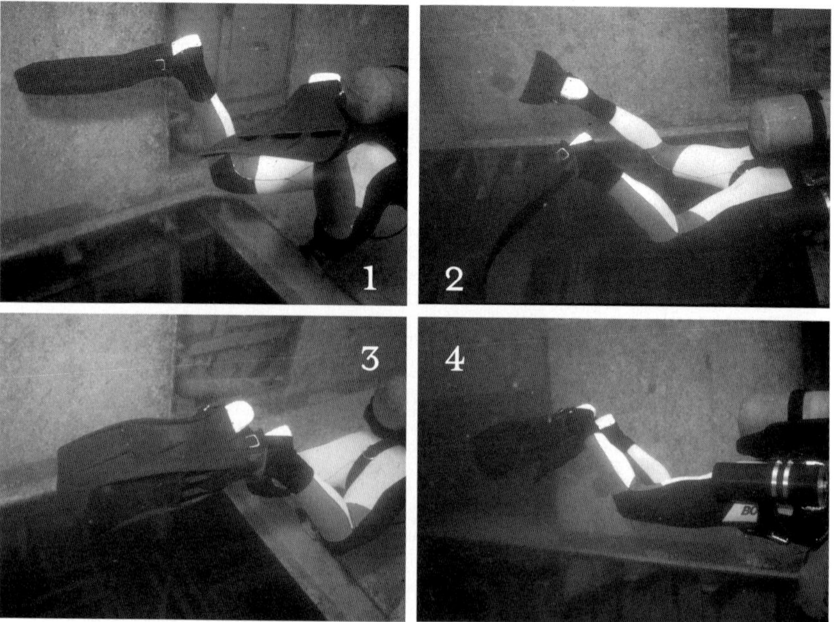

The frog kick allows the diver to direct propulsion away from the floor; ©Ron De Amorim

quires that one exercise greater control over their kicking style. The frog kick can be used as a fairly powerful kick in high flow conditions or curtailed in response to low flow areas with easily disturbed sediments. Because the frog kick allows the diver greater control of water movement and directs the water up and back rather than down, it usually creates less silt than alternative propulsion methods.

Directional Awareness

Different environments demand different types of navigational skill. So, while it is important that all divers cultivate basic navigational skills, it is equally important to augment these with specialized skills specific to the environment in which one does most of their diving. If one does not know where they are going, diving in the ocean can be equally as hazardous as diving in a cave, so it is important to cultivate the skills required by each. An excellent way of becoming aware of the navigational demands of a given area is to seek out local direction; when in doubt ask questions. To their detriment, divers frequently ignore dive briefings or are embarrassed to ask questions, often becoming lost before the dive even begins.

Do You Have Good Directional Awareness?

A. New Diver
- Good awareness of surroundings
- Ability to negotiate basic reciprocal and triangular compass courses
- Ability to dive from and locate an anchored dive boat
- Awareness of potential problems and risks within a particular dive

B. Advanced Diver
- Excellent awareness of surroundings, notice problems quickly or before they develop
- Proficiency with compass navigation
- Moderate experience in several environments such as night, overhead, and wreck
- Always clarify points of confusion in dive plan and restructure as necessary

C. Advanced Technical Diver
- Proficiency with compass navigation and basic survey techniques
- Proficient navigation in open water and technical diving settings
- Experienced diver in a variety of environments with cave, wreck, and gas training

- Do not dive until confident that dive plan is safe and understood by all teams

Buddy Skills

A diver is either completely dedicated to the buddy system—and all that it entails—or s/he is a bad dive buddy; there is really no middle ground here. Casual dive buddies can be a substantial liability, since poor buddy skills can result not only in lost divers but also in differing expectations. For example, a diver committed to the buddy system, and who finds him/herself separated from a team member, will usually spend the dive (usually at increasing personal risk) looking for someone who may feel comfortable leaving the water or diving area without informing anyone. Unfortunately, these kinds of situations have resulted in several tragic fatalities. Some divers shun the buddy system, claiming it is a practice relevant only to basic open water diving. However, this belief is unfounded, and exists largely because of a failure to recognize the advantages of a good dive buddy.

Good buddy skills improve safety and increase diving fun in all underwater environments.

©Sandra Edwards, Ft. Lauderdale

Some people assume that requiring a dive buddy is a sign of dependency. In fact, there is nothing further from the truth; good dive buddy skills not only promote diver awareness, they also promote ability. A capable dive buddy can be a tremendous asset, offering redundant equipment, an added perspective, more safety, and a source of greater enjoyment. If one derides the need for a dive buddy, because of bad dive buddy experiences, the latter are usually the result of either a poor emphasis on buddy skills or of unrefined diving skills. Like most worthwhile activities, buddy diving is an investment; this means that what dividends one reaps are directly proportional to how much time one spends developing good skills in themselves and their team.

How Are your buddy skills?

A. New Diver

- Review buddy's equipment and dive plan prior to dive
- Stay with dive buddy during entire dive and frequently check their personal status; learn to look for things like unusual bubbling or signs of stress
- Show good buddy skills by making it easy to be seen by one's buddy and by openly communicating problems, concerns, or personal limitations to him/her
- Have a basic understanding of rescue diving skills, of current first aid/CPR, and have access to all emergency phone numbers

B. Advanced Diver

- Always be completely familiar with dive buddy's equipment and review the equipment and configuration used by other divers in the area
- Review dive plan to be certain it is safe and well understood by all
- Dive with a watchful eye toward preventing problems before they develop
- Habitually check dive buddy and make it easy to be located by one's dive buddy (often with an underwater light that assists communication and location)
- Rescue diver certified with current first aid and CPR training
- Carry basic first aid kit and have access to all emergency numbers

C. Advanced Technical Diver

- Dive with people that are well versed in the DIR system but always be aware of other divers in the area and what problems they may cause
- Actively participate in the construction and dissemination of a safe and comprehensive dive plan while ensuring that all involved are comfortable and capable
- Instructor level awareness of dive buddy with automatic problem solving awareness; i.e., continually correcting issues before they become problems
- Rescue trained with current first aid and CPR, emergency first aid kit, and well versed in all evacuation and emergency plans
- Carry cell phone and/or other means of contacting emergency personnel
- Make contact with local emergency treatment areas and be familiar with procedures
- Contact hyperbaric facilities to ensure their ability to handle a diving related emergency

Communication

Communication is a central component of efficient team diving. On any particular dive, information that is either not relayed or poorly communicated can easily increase stress and/or risk. For example, an uncomfortable diver should be able to easily communicate his/her anxiety to any team member before a problem emerges, so that a solution can be mutually and quickly agreed upon.

In close quarters, with good visibility, communication between divers is usually fairly easy. Hand signals are the most common method of communication. When an idea is complicated or not being properly understood, divers should write the information on an underwater slate. Taking a few seconds to ensure proper communication can easily save time and possibly lives. However, because they allow for quick communication at close to moderate distances, all divers should be familiar with basic hand signals.

The following review outlines several of the most fundamental communication signals one is likely to encounter while diving. Divers should be familiar with these and with any others relevant to their local diving area. If one is diving with someone new, one must always review hand signals, as these can vary from area to area and from diver to diver. Frequent dive buddies often employ an extensive list of signals, with some going as far as communicating in sign language.

I. Hand Signals

A. OK: Like other command signals, the OK sign must be returned

©Wes Sadler

The thumbs up signal means "Terminate the Dive."

with an affirmation or an indication of the problem. Remember, if a diver is having a problem, it is their responsibility to inform the team. If another diver is having a problem, then they can use this query as an opportunity to convey the problem.

B. Stop/Hold: Failure to properly recognize and acknowledge the stop or hold command can be very dangerous. Misunderstandings relating to the hold signal have resulted in confusion and fatalities. The stop com-

This hand signal can be used as a question or a statement: "Are you OK?", "Yes, I'm OK."

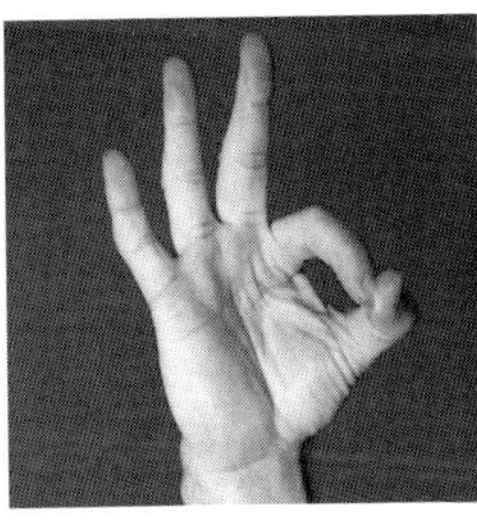

This command signal means "Hold." It must be answered with a return "Hold" signal. not an "OK."

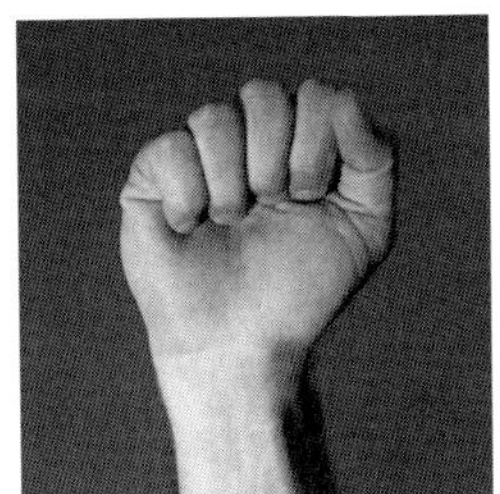

mand is communicated with a closed fist directed toward the other diver(s). The open palm signal is also common in the open water community. It is crucial that this command be returned, as a miscommunication could easily lead to team separation.

C. Call The Dive: Divers use the thumbs up signal to terminate a dive. This signal often indicates that some limit has been reached, e.g., of a gas supply. However, it may also indicate that a diver is uncomfortable and wants to exit the area.

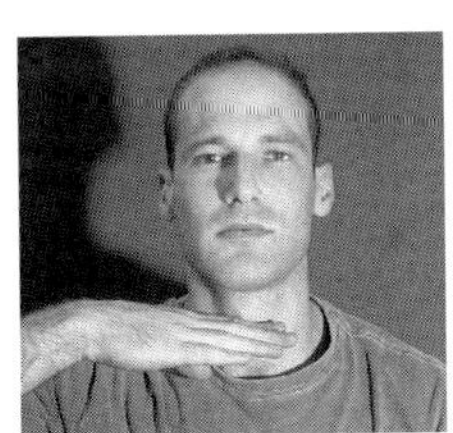

The emergency signal for "Out of Air" demands an immediate response.

D. Out of Air: As indicated in the above figure, the out-of-air signal is given by drawing the hand across the throat. This is an emergency signal and demands immediate attention. Upon receiving it, team members should prepare to donate air. Divers using lights can signal team members, shortening the delay response time.

E. Safety Stop: It is recommended that on any dive, regardless of decompression obligation, divers make at least a three-minute safety stop. Safety or decompression stops can be indicated in several ways. The two most common are to hold a fist in front of the diver and raise the pinkie. Another popular method is to hold out an open hand with the palm down and motion parallel to the ground back and forth from the chest in a repetitive fashion, indicating a stop.

F. Low on Air: Divers that are low on air should indicate this to fellow members and then terminate the dive. Placing one's closed fist on one's sternum, palm towards the chest, achieves this.

G. Silt: The disturbance of bottom sediments, i.e., silt, can be indicated with a palm down gesture while rubbing the thumb across the ends of one's fingers. A diver may choose to use this signal to communicate to a team member that they are disturbing the bottom or to warn them of an upcoming silty area. Silting is nearly always the result of poor technique and, with practice, can be corrected. In an attempt to improve performance and reduce silt, divers should always communicate poor technique to their team members.

H. Line, Line Tangle, Cutting the Line: The index finger crossed over the middle finger is the common signal that represents a line. A diver may communicate more specific information about the line using this signal in conjunction with others. For example, the line sign done with the hand moving in a figure eight pattern denotes a line entanglement, while the line signal pointed downward and rotating indicates a line tie off or placement. This same signal can also be moved in a circular pattern, which represents the action of winding a reel and seeks to communicate the reeling in of the line. Fingers moved in a cutting action alternated with the line sign indicate the cutting of a line.

I. Bubbles: To indicate the presence of bubbles, a diver should hold out one hand and bring their index finger down to their thumb in a repetitive motion; the distance between index finger and thumb should increase to indicate larger bubbles. With this signal, a diver can easily point out to a team member that a hose or regulator is bubbling. Bubbles coming from a diver's valve-regulator orifice often indicate the need for a new o-ring.

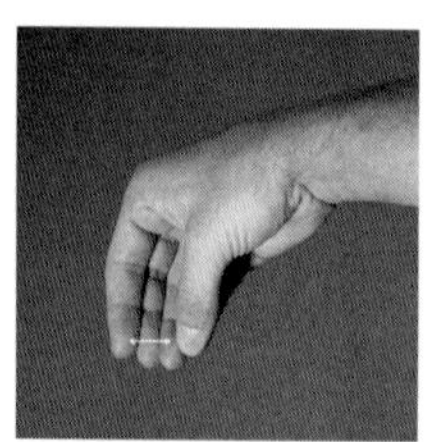
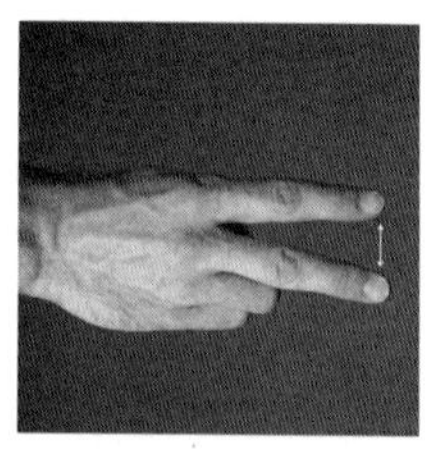

The hand signals for "Bubbles," "Silt" and "Cut" or "Cut the Line."

Numerical Hand Signals

ONE

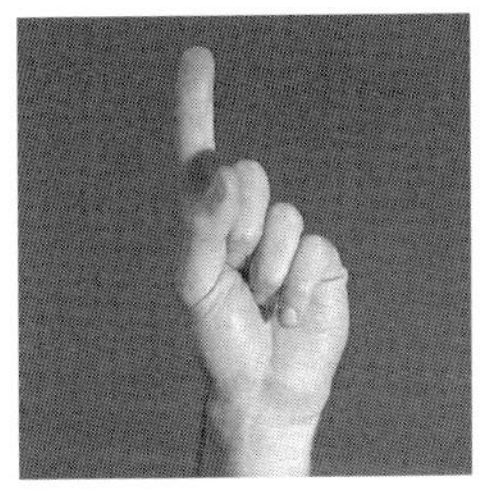

SIX

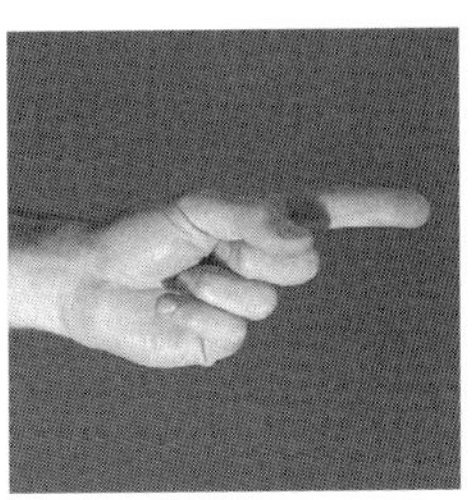

TWO

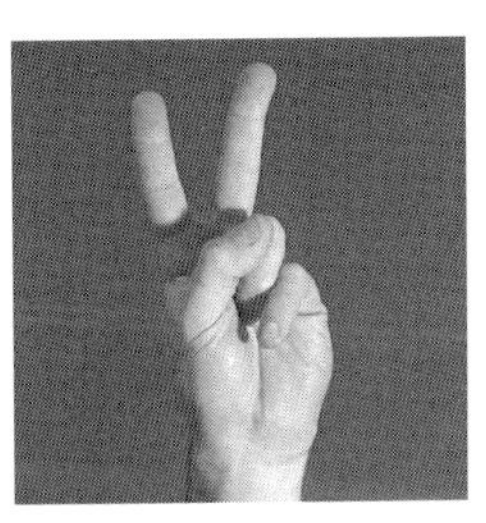

SEVEN

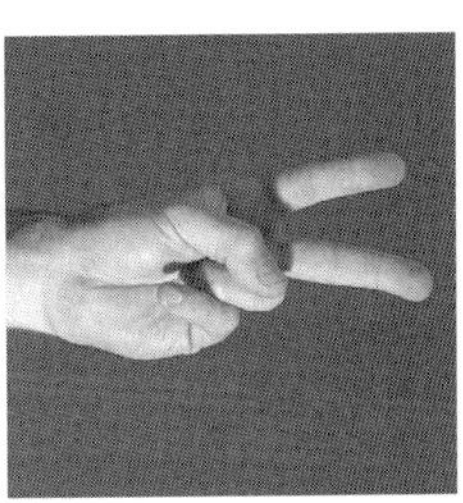

THREE

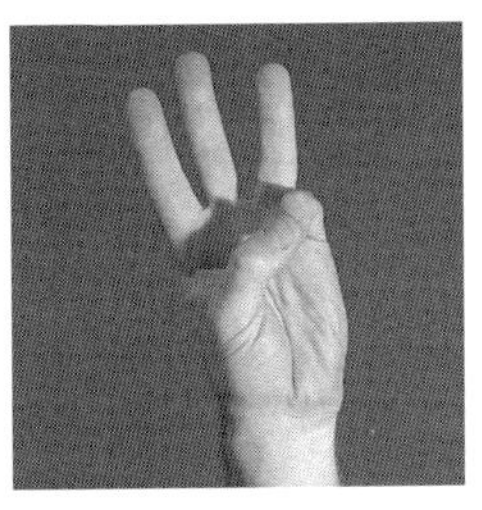

EIGHT

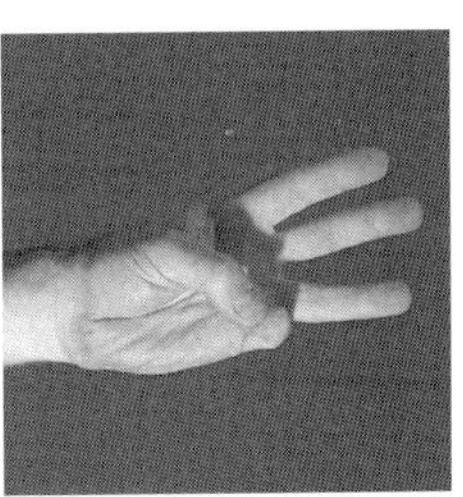

FOUR

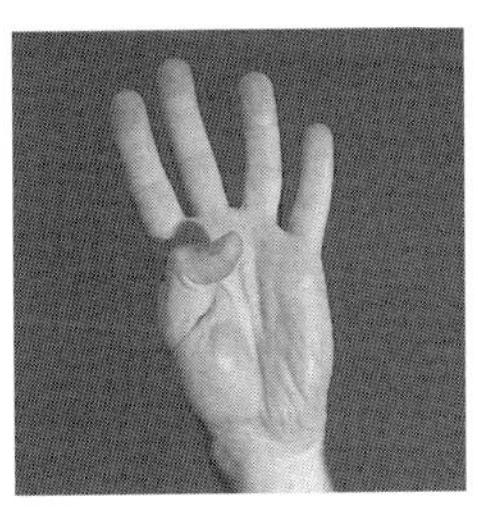

NINE

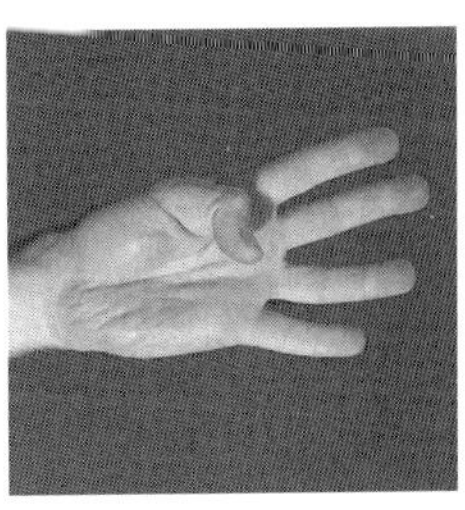

FIVE

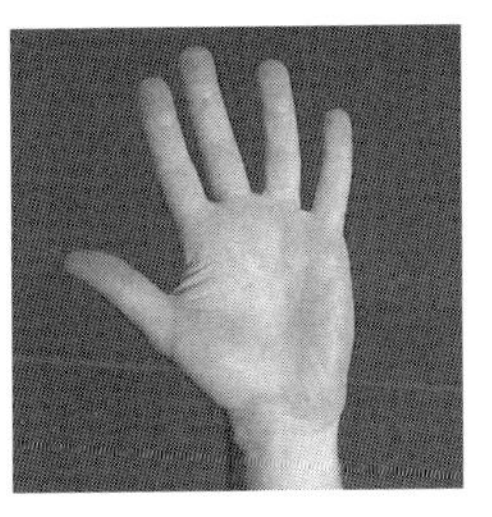

TEN

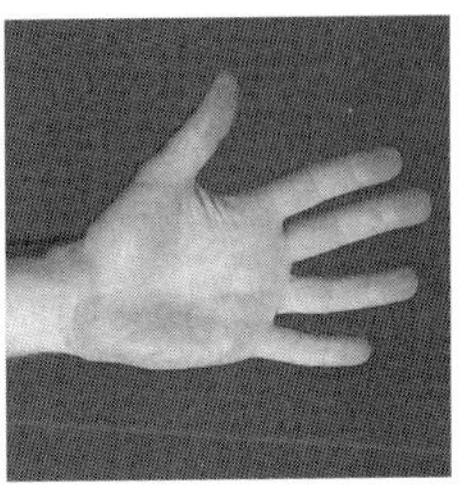

II. Light Signals

Light signals can be an important means of communication because they work in a variety of situations and are especially effective in gaining a team member's attention. In dark surroundings, individuals can easily communicate with their lights over large distances. Even in close quarters light signals may be preferable, especially if divers are not facing one another. Many open water divers are starting to realize how lights can simplify communication and enrich a dive.

Divers frequently use light signals over hand signals because they are:

- Easy to see
- More efficient to use
- Effective at much greater distances

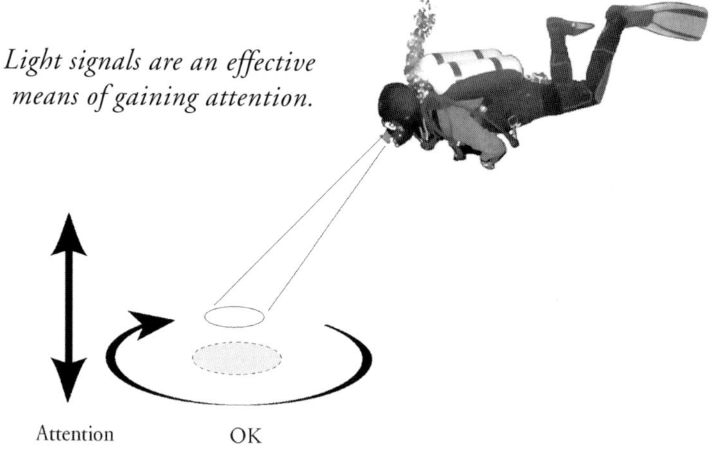

Light signals are an effective means of gaining attention.

A. OK: A slowly circling light indicates OK and can be used either to ask a diver if they are OK or to answer a question. Avoid shining the light in anyone's eyes. Generally, pointing the light at the floor, and drawing a circle with the beam there, is sufficient for communication and to prevent blinding one's dive buddy.

B. Attention vs. Emergency: Rapid light signals indicate a problem and demand immediate attention. In contrast to a purposeful side to side or up and down motion with one's light, which indicates attention, a rapid light signal, denotes an emergency. In a real emergency the diver should move their light rapidly from side to side (or up and down) until the diver being signalled turns to assist. Once the signalled diver turns, the light should be diverted so as not to blind them. The attention gesture is a far more common signal. Indeed, an air failure is the most likely cause for the emergency signal; therefore, its use should prepare the responding diver for an impending air sharing occurrence. Erratic light signals should be avoided unless one is truly in need of immediate assistance.

III. Touch Contact: Zero Visibility

During a loss of visibility, light and hand signals become useless, and divers must resort to physical contact to communicate with one another. During touch contact, divers will take hold of their dive buddy, usually an arm or a leg; this will depend on the size of the cave. In this situation, a system of rudimentary commands has been established to allow for efficient communication; one, continuous, firm squeeze means *stop*, a forward push means *move forward*, and a backward tug means *back up*. Crossing the index and middle finger, and jamming it in a dive buddy's hand, twisting them back and forth, can communicate a *line entanglement*.

Equipment Management

Divers must be able to manage their equipment in a comfortable and efficient manner. Individuals that are not comfortable with their equipment can waste valuable time trying to manage the simplest of situations. For example, divers that are not efficient at passing a regulator to an out-of-air diver increase the stress and danger of an already dangerous situation. Generally speaking, divers with poor equipment familiarity experience more stress than others, and also do not perform well as dive buddies.

Divers with poor equipment handling skills are usually the result of unexacting training programs and of rushed certification processes. It is important that, before moving onto more aggressive diving conditions, one masters the requisite skills and equipment specific to each level of certification. Shortcuts in diver training or in proficiency reduce enjoyment, increase stress and put lives at risk.

How Well Do You Manage Your Equipment?

A. New Diver

- Divers should be able to easily assemble and disassemble their diving equipment
- Divers should be knowledgeable in the cleaning and basic maintenance of their equipment
- Divers should easily be able to check their breathing supply, clear

their mask, and reach other basic equipment
- Divers should be able to remove and replace their equipment while underwater (shallow) and at the surface

B. Advanced Diver
- Divers should be familiar with the assembly, maintenance, and function of all their equipment
- Divers should be able to maintain basic items such as tank o-rings and light bulbs
- While floating horizontally divers should be able to check their breathing supply, clear their mask and reach other basic equipment
- Proficiency with lift-bags and other surface markers
- Divers should be able to comfortably doff and don equipment in less than two minutes while under water and at the surface
- Divers should be able to remove a dive buddy's equipment at the surface in less than one minute

C. Advanced Technical Diver
- Understand and maintain the fundamental components of their diving system
- Proficiency with all lift devices and environment specific items such as guideline devices
- Be able to clear debris from a clogged second stage
- Be able to fix items such as o-rings on tanks and hoses
- Divers should be able to doff entire technical rig at the surface in less than one minute
- Divers should be able to remove a dive buddy's equipment at the surface in under one minute

Divers must resort to touch contact communication when hand and light signals become useless due to total loss of visibility.

©Wes Sadler

Investing energy in proper training, efficient configurations and sound diving principles allows divers the opportunity to engage in a variety of exciting diving opportunities.

©GUE Kea, Greece

Streamlining and efficiency should be second nature by the time you are combining deep ocean scootering, underwater videography, and drift decompression techniques.

Chapter 4

DIR Philosophy

Poor Technique Is A Real Drag

Streamlining is an important consideration to a whole variety of activities, ranging from running and biking to the manufacturing of cars and airplanes. The sports world is keenly aware of the value of streamlining, with a great deal of time and effort spent trying to reduce the slightest resistance created by helmets, clothing, and even the laces on running shoes. In the case of water-based activities, e.g., swimming and diving, the increased density of water, with its associated drag and turbulence, forces one to take into account issues of streamlining in order to find the most efficient way of moving through the water. For example, competitive swimmers wear special suits designed to reduce the turbulence created by their own skin. It is no wonder, then, that streamlining is an essential component of efficient and comfortable diving.

It is ironic, then, that SCUBA divers are rarely aware of how much minor amounts of drag increase their stress and effort. Consider this: resistance increases as the square of velocity. To overcome this resistance, the energy required increases approximately as the cube of the initial energy required. What this means is that if one doubles the surface area of something, this results in a resistance that is four times the original resistance; in turn, this requires an increase in energy nearly sixteen times as great to offset the increase in resistance. Conversely, if a diver reduces his/her surface area, s/he will derive substantial benefits in the form of reduced effort and stress. A diver's choices then are clear; one can either

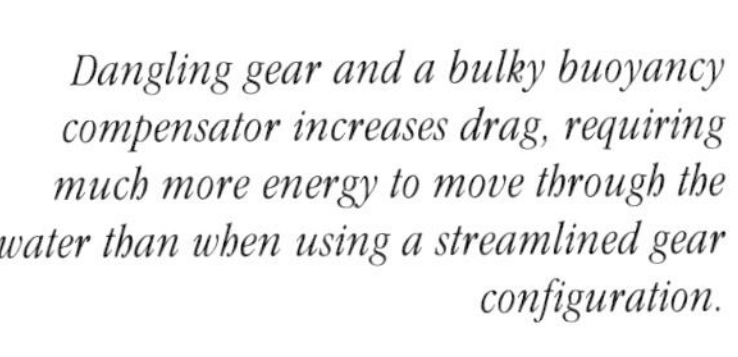

Dangling gear and a bulky buoyancy compensator increases drag, requiring much more energy to move through the water than when using a streamlined gear configuration.

©GUE

reduce what drag their own equipment causes or invest substantially greater effort into inefficient movement through the water. Allowing equipment to dangle, or investing in bulky buoyancy compensators, obviously increases one's drag, and those who opt for these also commit themselves to a gratuitous waste of energy. The geometric impact of poor streamlining means, then, that educated divers have at their disposal an obvious and simple method for radically reducing the stress of their dives, a fact which makes all the more ironic the casual addition of unnecessary drag—in the form of unfortunate equipment choices—opted for by many current divers.

Doing-It-Right

The Doing-It-Right (DIR) system of diving provides divers, new and old, with a clear alternative to inefficient and unsafe diving practices. DIR is an holistic system, a system that blends an emphasis on safety with the world's most robust equipment configuration. DIR is internationally renowned for its success, simplicity, and safety. Though people generally focus on the revolutionary impact it has had on equipment configuration, appreciating the enhancements it offers, it would be shortsighted to view DIR equipment considerations in isolation from its founding principles. This is because DIR is a system; it realizes a way of thinking that seeks to intensify diving enjoyment by enhancing efficiency and safety. Simply put, DIR is a diving philosophy that promotes rational choices with respect to dive teams, dive preparation, and equipment configuration as a means of ensuring safety, efficiency, and enjoyment. The DIR system incorporates the general categories of the unified team, preparation, and building a dive plan.

I. Unified Team

A dive team is not an arbitrary collection of individuals but a group that acts with the team's interest in mind. Each member must first be independently capable or they will only burden the buddy team. The adage that a chain is only as strong as the weakest link is very appropriate in this setting. Divers have an obligation to inform the team when dives are beyond their ability or when their sphere of comfort has been exceeded. Diving related problems often result from the accumulation of several poorly managed problems, often the result of poor dive buddy skills and/or irresponsible team members.

Team diving is an important part of any type of diving. Divers should frequently reference one another, remaining prepared to assist a team member with any difficulties before they become a problem. Asserting the value of team diving does not detract from the need for individual competence. On the contrary, team members should be individually capable of undertaking a given dive, thereby increasing the safety of the team as a whole. Divers that are less capable can bring the team to a lower level of proficiency and compromise team safety. Therefore, dive plans should cater to the weakest diver. Teams should also choose their members carefully, particularly in demanding diving environments.

Buddy separation is a common component of diving emergencies and diver fatalities. Separation from one's diving buddy is almost always due to careless diving. In shallow water recreational diving, individuals are instructed to search for one minute and then surface. However, in

Diving with qualified dive buddies is much safer and far more rewarding than diving alone. Right, three divers enjoying a shallow recreational reef dive with scooters.

©Sandra Edwards, Ft. Lauderdale

most forms of technical diving (deep, decompression obligation, overhead), this is not feasible. Regardless of the environment, divers functioning together in a team are less likely to experience problems and are substantially more prepared to manage unforeseen difficulties. Astute divers will rarely, if ever, become separated from a dive buddy. Divers can stay together more easily by remaining aware during the dive and checking buddy location frequently.

Good diver awareness and proper diving procedures should be able to prevent diver separation. Team diving is greatly facilitated by special diving equipment such as powerful underwater lights. These lights make it much easier for teams to stay together and to communicate with one another. Even in the open ocean, lights that are 30 watts or greater allow for significant communication and can provide a dive buddy with an excellent visual reference. Divers can move through the water referencing one another on a regular basis, and by passing the light across their buddy's visual field (not in the face), providing a constant source of reference. Divers that make it easy for others to stay with them will enjoy much greater team support and comfort. Of course, it is possible to dive alone, but team diving with qualified dive buddies is much safer and far more rewarding. Dive teams can relay important information to each other regarding individual diving technique, point out features that others may miss, prevent troubles before they occur, and assist in emergency situations. Individuals that view team diving in a negative

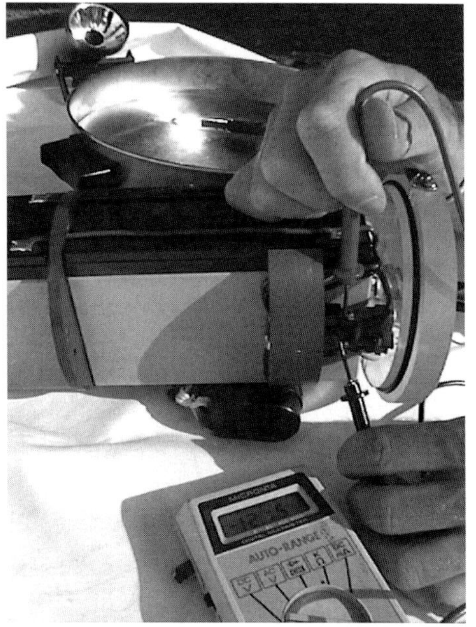

Burn testing a light's battery is part of regular maintenance to ensure sufficient longetivity and proper operation.

Proper gear maintenance must be an ongoing commitment, not something to be performed immediately prior to diving.

©Anthony Rue

light have never enjoyed the benefit of a good dive buddy.

II. PREPARATION

A. Pre-dive Preparation: Far too many divers assume that pre-dive preparation begins the day or even hours before the dive. True pre-dive preparation is an ongoing commitment involving three essential components: mental focus, physical fitness and diving experience. Divers who try to circumvent any of these are not truly prepared for the dive, and may experience reduced comfort, a missed dive opportunity, or even a hazardous situation.

B. Mental Focus: Divers who are not focused on the dive cannot be responsive to a dive buddy or to the demands made on them by their surroundings. Good mental focus not only allows divers to truly enjoy dives, but it also enables them to remain aware of their surroundings while being prepared to intervene before problems escalate. On the other hand, poor focus often leads to problems. For example, by losing focus on a dive, a team can miss proper air supply turn points, drift into dangerous areas, or separate. Proper awareness consistently increases the safety, efficiency and enjoyment of all diving activities.

C. Physical Fitness: Unfit individuals are subject to an increased risk of disease and experience shorter lives of lesser quality. Furthermore, unfit divers are much more likely to suffer from diving related problems; for example, unfit divers are not only at a greater risk of decompression illness (DCI), they are also less capable of overcoming the demands of a stressful situation. They not only place themselves at risk, they also place at risk other team members who may be called upon to help them in a crisis.

Fitness includes cardiovascular health, strength, flexibility, nutrition, abstinence from smoking and drug use, and limited or nonexistent alcohol consumption. Overweight and/or out of shape divers should take responsibility for their lives and adopt an effective regime of diet and exercise. At a minimum, divers should average four days per week of cardiovascular exercise lasting at least 30 minutes and avoid high fat, high cholesterol diets, focusing instead on a generous consumption of fruits, vegetables and grains.

D. Diving Experience: Extensive "technical" dives conducted by groups such as GUE or WKPP may give the impression that long range or deep dives can be accomplished with relative ease. For example, world record dives have now become commonplace as GUE and the WKPP continue to extend the exploration of Wakulla Springs cave system by thousands of feet each dive. Accomplishments of this sort not only prepare these groups for even greater achievements, they also allow other teams to incorporate these ideas and practices into their operations, thereby augmenting their own abilities. However, divers should remember that

WKPP divers regularly participate in continuing dive education seminars.

©Jarrod Jablonski

these feats have been the result of years of preparation and cumulative experience; and if, in their diving, divers ignore the experience factor that goes into successfully accomplishing these feats, they will put themselves at very great risk.

E. Dive Planning: The rewards and hazards of every diving venture require that the dive team develop a comprehensive, yet flexible, dive plan well in advance of their entry into the water. Contrary to what the term "dive planning" might suggest, dive planning involves much more than simply laying out a path for a dive team to follow. A dive team equipped with a dive plan is much more capable of dealing with unexpected challenges, preventing small problems from mushrooming into serious ones, and is more likely to enjoy their dive. Testing equipment, reviewing emergency procedures and finalizing the dive plan prior to entering the water, all help prevent the majority of problems from ever occurring.

i. Prior to the Trip: The first aspect to any dive trip is the information gathering process. One must first pick a desired site and then gather information on it. For example, what season is the best to dive this site? What season is the worst? What kind of equipment does this site require? What level of experience? If divers who lack the requisite experience accompany the group, is there anything else for them to do? Additionally, divers should seek to establish whether there are suitable and available accommodations nearby and whether the transportation requirements are clear and well organized. One should also evaluate what equipment and spare parts the trip requires and whether, and what cost, this can be either rented or purchased. Having the information one needs before traveling to a far away location can greatly help ensure that a dive experience will be a truly positive one. This information could then be used to formulate a comprehensive dive plan, one discussed below.

ii. Arriving at the Dive Site: Divers should always conduct a general site survey. This will hopefully verify pre-trip information and may involve evaluation of boat diving or land-based excursions. During this survey, the team should also verify water conditions, diving logistics, and emergency procedures. On land-based excursions divers should choose entrances that are convenient and which provide a reduced risk of spoiling visibility or of damaging the environment. In addition, divers should choose a convenient location to assemble their equipment. Equipment is usually easier to carry when assembled and transported on one's back.

iii. Prior to the Dive: Following the general site survey, the team should assemble their equipment, usually leaving suit donning for last. The team should then discuss what equipment it will need, ensure that all members agree upon placement, and check for equipment failures. At this time, lights and regulators should be checked for functionality, while items like reels or lift bags should be examined to see if they are in good working order. Furthermore, this is the time when the team should discuss the dive plan in detail and its members verify that everyone is comfortable with the proposed dive. Remember that all dives must take into account the diver with the least experience, and should avoid plans that are too goal-oriented or which fixate the team on a single objective.

Teamwork extends to all portions of the dive, including pre-dive planning. Right, GUE representatives Todd Kincaid and Tamara Kendel prepare for a research dive in Bimini, Bahamas.

©Anthony Rue

III. Building a Dive Plan

The following dive planning outline should help divers identify the key components of a sound dive plan. Coupled with individual experience, this outline will facilitate dive planning in a wide range of environments. Obviously, individuals preparing for dives in new environments must use this information alongside information gleaned from local authorities, personal experience, and common sense.

A. Define Dive Objectives: Goal oriented diving is a reality in most forms of diving; to pretend otherwise merely confuses safe dive preparation. Goals can be as simple as enjoying a shallow reef or as complex as exploring miles of new cave. In itself, goal oriented diving is not a problem; by remaining aware of their limitations and of the risks of the dive planned, divers can prevent their desire to achieve a certain goal from undermining what common sense and realistic dive parameters dictate. However, if divers become obsessed with achieving a particular goal, to the exclusion of what safe diving parameters dictate, the risks associated with goal oriented diving increase dramatically. For example, a diver focused on getting to a certain point in a cave might ignore or cheat on their designated gas supply, placing themselves and the team at greater risk. Therefore, it is important that divers acknowledge what they hope

Making the dive plan includes defining dive objectives, defining risk, the logistics of the dive, and establishing parameters such as time and depth. Right, clockwise from lower left: Jarrod Jablonski, Todd Kincaid, Barry Miller, and Per Anderson before a dive on the Titanic's sister ship, the HMS Britannic.

©GUE, Kea, Greece

to get out of the dive and agree beforehand that anytime a stated objective compromises team safety, that objective must be abandoned.

B. Define Risk: Few concepts are as relative to the specific desires and abilities of individuals as is the concept of acceptable risk. In both their lives and in their diving, people differ widely on what they accept as a permissible level of risk. For some, very little risk is acceptable, for others, the greater the risk, the more attractive a given enterprise. With respect to dive planning, it is not only important that dive team members agree on what constitutes an acceptable level of risk; they must also share about the same level of proficiency. For divers with limited skill, shallow reef diving can be more dangerous than a deep cave dive will be for others who have the requisite skill and experience. All diving activity has a component of risk, and oftentimes it is relative to one's experience.

In dive planning, team members should work towards identifying the objective risks of a given dive and seek to minimize exposing divers to unnecessary peril. In other words, they should recognize the true risks of a given dive and assess whether the risks inherent to the planned dive (e.g., overhead or decompression) are acceptable.

In fact, if performed correctly, most common diving involves very low levels of risk. However, lack of diver proficiency, poor planning, and the careless use of advanced technology, elevates the risk of an otherwise simple diving activity. Usually the risk of a particular dive has less to do with the dive itself than it has to do with the planning, ability, and experience of its participants. In short, people generally create their own problems by not properly managing or identifying the true risks of the dive.

C. Diving Logistics: Diving logistics primarily concern the manner in which a diver experiences a dive site and the methods that will govern that experience. While cave divers usually operate from a car, others travel to dive sites in boats, as is the case in ocean and lake diving. Other logistical considerations may involve additional technical support, such as underwater propulsion vehicles.

The logistics of a particular dive can vary substantially from one location to the next. Nonetheless, the common parameters of planning that seek to maximize safety will include sufficient amounts of support, of gas, and sound contingency and emergency measures. In many cases, a diving leader undertakes to do a great deal of logistical planning; this oftentimes leads individuals into a false sense of security that lacks a true

Filming a dive can be a complex task requiring careful planning, whether for an Imax feature film or a personal video of a Carribean reef.

©Jarrod Jablonski

©David Rhea, Bimini

appreciation for dive planning or risk.

D. Establish Parameters: Diving parameters can include an array of limitations that vary in their relevance to any given dive. The risk of a particular dive is often greatly magnified (if not created) by the lack or avoidance of appropriate diving parameters. Reports of fatal accidents are filled with divers who failed to establish sensible limitations or who ignored established parameters, resulting in insufficient breathing gas, extended decompression obligation, or team and/or support vessel separation.

i. Time: Individuals must define the period of the day during which they will conduct their diving activities and agree upon acceptable bottom times. Certain dives (e.g., ocean dives) might have to be cancelled if it becomes too late, since the difficulties associated with finding a team lost at sea increase exponentially with reduced ambient light. Because caves are largely subject to static conditions, safe cave diving does not usually require accounting for time of day. However, considerations of team safety require that all parameters—including time limitations—be established with the worst-case scenario in mind.

Bottom time limitations will be largely contingent on the experience of team members, the diving environment, and the time of day established for diving activity. For example, for divers uncomfortable with decompression, the planned diving depth will preset their exposure limit. Decompression divers, on the other hand,

Part of dive planning is accounting for contingencies such as becoming separated from the support vessel.

©Halcyon

will be limited by what are considered to be acceptable decompression times. Divers that are new to decompression should proceed progressively, adding longer decompression times as they become more comfortable.

Environmental instability (e.g., in ocean diving) also limits both what counts as a reasonable bottom time and what constitutes an acceptable decompression exposure. Because of the many potential risks to team safety associated with sudden environmental change (e.g., weather, shipping lane traffic or current), dives in the ocean should generally not exceed ninety minutes of total immersion. Cave divers rarely have to contend with these issues; personal comfort is typically the limiting factor here.

Decompression diving in the open ocean can be more challenging than in a more controlled environment.

©Steve Berman, Kea, Greece

The length of a particular dive can also be impacted by other factors, e.g., by thermal requirements, DPV burn times, breathing supplies, and lighting requirements. For example, when cave diving, divers should leave a 20% reserve on primary lighting requirements while making sure that each of their two back-up lights should enable them to exit from the spot of their maximum penetration. Furthermore, divers should be very familiar with their DPV battery power and ensure that they can return to safety in the event of a DPV failure.

ii. *Depth:* The expression "deep diving" is meaningless outside the context of individual experience and team preparedness. However, dives exceeding 100 fsw (30 msw) require progressively greater levels of experience and preparation. Beyond (and in many cases near) 100 fsw (30 msw), divers should use helium based mixtures to eliminate the effects of narcotic impairment. To try and go beyond these depths on air is irresponsible and fraught with greatly elevated risk; given what we know today, deep air diving can create a reckless and unnecessary risk.

Mixed gas diving has all but eliminated the most obvious risk to deep diving, and has greatly reduced the risk faced by most sensible divers. Nonetheless, deeper diving creates its own set of risks, including extended decompression obligations, time limitations, breathing gas supply, and ascent limitations. Deeper diving is similar to overhead diving in that divers cannot simply go to the surface to resolve problems. Therefore, divers that engage in deep diving must be well informed in the mechanics of decompression diving and be prepared to manage problems efficiently. Deeper dives also require more careful attention to established time limits, as a matter of minutes can result in exponential increases in decompression and problems in breathing supply requirements. Many divers have created insurmountable obstacles for themselves by extending their bottom time at depth without accounting for reserve supplies or contingency plans.

E. Establish Responsibility: All dives require that tasks be conducted for the fun and safety of the entire diving group. In some cases, one diver is responsible for tasks that benefit the whole group, e.g., towing a surface float or running a guideline in the overhead; in others, each team member is the bearer of their own responsibilities, e.g., air management and team unity. Regardless of individual or team responsibilities, divers should be able to function in all necessary capacities.

F. Contingency Planning: Properly crafted dive plans always account for contingencies. Unscheduled extensions in bottom time, greater decompression obligations, separation from a diving support vessel or a team need to be accounted for when formulating a dive plan. Contingency planning should always include a preparedness to address emergency situations such as decompression sickness, lost divers, and other medical

Researcher Gene Hobbs at the hyperbaric chamber control panel within Duke's Center for Hyperbaric Medicine.

emergencies.

G. Equipment: All divers should be very familiar with individual, team, and emergency equipment. Leading explorers long ago recognized that true familiarity with another diver's equipment was difficult without standardized configurations. Team standardization is another substantial benefit to DIR diving because divers are already familiar with one another's equipment.

H. Nutritional Requirements: Unfortunately, most divers ignore proper nutrition, especially while on a dive trip. Diving activities can lead to fatigue, and if badly nourished, a diver might find him/herself in a difficult situation if sudden, heavy, exertion is required, e.g., if one has to swim against a strong current to get to the boat. Individuals should be well nourished and especially well hydrated before diving.

The Duke Center for Hyperbaric Medicine's Atlantis diving bell was used in 1981 for what was, at that time, the world's deepest dive, 2250 FSW.

©GUE

Chapter 5

An Overview of the DIR Equipment Configuration

In contrast to all its other elements, it is the DIR equipment configuration that tends to generate the majority of interest and debate. This focus on equipment has produced the misconception that one can selectively embrace one part of the system, e.g., correct equipment configuration, while ignoring the others. For example, some endorse the DIR equipment configuration, but ignore essential aspects such as the team-centered approach or issues of physical fitness. This is a mistake; DIR is an holistic system. Although incorporating parts of the DIR system into another system will certainly benefit the latter, the result is ultimately neither desirable nor DIR. Furthermore, this hybrid is also likely to be fraught with complications.

Neither GUE nor DIR recommend measures that do not maximize a diver's efficiency. However, neither concept precludes learning and evolution. In fact, GUE heavily encourages this process. For example, divers that eliminate dragging gauges but continue to use a bulky open water buoyancy compensator have made an important improvement encouraged by DIR concepts. However, such changes are still not in keeping with DIR's fundamental principles, which provide for maximum efficiency. The problem with the evolutionary DIR approach is that people evaluate the system by looking at dissociated parts and are never able to fully appreciate the complete DIR philosophy. Partial solutions are improvements upon an existing configuration, but DIR ultimately prescribes the most efficient system. While a transition to DIR is beneficial, the incomplete shift to DIR techniques results in wasted time, unnecessary effort, and reduced diving fun.

This "all or nothing" view is also relevant to considerations surrounding the equipment configuration itself. Divers who opt to make changes to any part of the configuration are likely to upset the carefully arranged components that are structured to complement one another. For example, one salient tenet of the DIR system is that of passing the regulator from one's mouth to an out-of-air diver; this ensures that the out-of-air diver receives a fully functioning regulator in the most expedient manner possible. Though some divers embrace this tenet, they, nonetheless, ignore other core components of the system. Such a "selective" approach clearly clashes with the fundamental principles of the DIR system. Divers using the same clean, well thought out configuration are safer and more able to assist one another. Changes to that system, however seemingly slight, invariably create complications.

The DIR system was carefully designed to work in all situations, not just in the long range, mixed gas, cave penetrations for which it is renowned. Extreme range exploratory divers long ago realized that a complicated system would compound difficulties, and that equipment had to facilitate their efforts, not complicate them. The same can be said for any diver or any situation. Unfortunately, most discussions about the system have focused on its use in long range cave dives. The truth is, however, that the DIR system is amazingly flexible and can be used in caves, in the ocean, in wrecks and under ice. It is ideal for relaxing reef dives at 30 feet, for extended penetration cave dives, as well as for difficult wreck dives. It is the perfect system in zero visibility as well as in crystal clear water.

The DIR system requires no modification in order to function effectively and efficiently in different environments. In fact, the system was not developed exclusively as a cave diving system; therefore, the issues it addresses are far from cave-specific. DIR owes its flexibility to careful research and development dives in diverse conditions including: the Baltic Sea, the Red Sea, the Mediterranean Sea, the Atlantic Ocean, the Pacific Ocean, the Great Lakes, the Puget Sound, and the St. Lawrence Seaway. Cold-water DIR divers use gloves and dry suits inflated with argon. In freezing water these divers use dry gloves and thicker undergarments with argon and possibly electric heat. Cold water divers use slightly larger bolt-snaps. Otherwise, exactly the same system is employed whether the dive is below the ice or in the balmy tropics.

DIR vs. Other Equipment "Styles"

Recently, some have tried to respond to the popularity of DIR by advocating other "systems." These configurations, however, are not really systems; they are, rather, a collection of loose recommendations put together from a variety of sources (often from the DIR system itself). It would be wise for divers to be wary of these, since such modifications compromise the fundamental efficiency and safety of DIR.

Since there are no other completely standardized systems in recreational or technical diving, it is really impossible to compare the DIR system to other styles. Nonetheless, some attempts at a comparison are made in what follows.

The Doing It Right System

The DIR system is based on the concept of minimalism. Equipment that does not enrich the dive is considered a liability and therefore to be left at home. DIR divers use a rigid back plate with a one-piece, webbed harness, a back-mounted buoyancy compensator for streamlined movement and horizontal posture, a short reserve hose that hangs around the neck for easy retrieval, and a hose from which they breathe that can be passed in the event of an emergency. In most situations this latter hose is longer in length (5-7 ft. or 1.5-2 m) than the former and runs under a hip-mounted light canister, is tucked in the belt, or is run under a waist mounted knife pouch. Though there are numerous other important elements forming the DIR system—we will address these in the next chapter—this simple configuration is the foundation of DIR.

The DIR system is a minimalist system: clean, streamlined and carefully designed to work for all types of diving.

©Ron De Amorim, Ft. Lauderdale

The Bungee Style—Donating from One's Retaining Device

This style places the backup hose in some type of surgical tubing or restrictive band. This band is placed on the side of the tanks, along the manifold or on the back plate. Divers who use a long hose (usually 5-7 ft. or 1.5-2 m) on their backup regulator usually "stuff" this hose during the equipment assembly portion of the dive. Opinion on where and how to secure the second stage of the long hose varies among these divers, adding further complications to this style. By stuffing the hose in some piece of bungee, it is more difficult to deploy, may not remain properly stowed, and will not be guaranteed to function (as will the regulator from one's mouth). Furthermore, without assistance, most divers are unable to return this hose to the "stowed" position; this not only makes them dependent upon a dive buddy to do so, it also creates complications in the event of an accidental deployment or an air share false alarm. Due to its inefficient operation and increased risk, most divers have given up on this system and prefer to donate the regulator in their mouth to an out-of-air diver.

DIR—Donating from One's Mouth

Donating the regulator that one is breathing from guarantees that the person most in need of a fully functioning regulator is going to get it. Any other regulator passed to an out-of-air diver may contain sand or other debris and may not function properly. In many out-of-air situations air-starved divers will simply pull the regulator from the donor's mouth; this means that divers who are practiced and prepared for this eventuality will likely respond more comfortably. The DIR system focuses on helping the diver in trouble by believing that any competent diver will want to facilitate a safe rescue. Even if the out-of-air diver remains calm and requests air with the proper signal, under the DIR system their first breath is guaranteed to be an effective one, as it comes from the regulator with which a diver was just breathing.

What About Open Water Diving?

Some people mistakenly assume that DIR is a system exclusively designed for technical diving. As the DIR system evolved, practitioners found themselves frustrated by having to return to their standard open

Donating one's primary regulator ensures that the out-of-air diver will receive a working regulator with the correct gas.

water configurations. Conventional open water equipment included loose fitting jacket style BC's, dangling gauges and bulky consoles. In addition, many open water divers are taught to donate air from a second stage that is hidden in a pocket or dangled carelessly behind. These systems are prone to excess drag and do not properly anticipate how to best respond to a troubled diver. Therefore, divers started using the DIR system in recreational open water situations and immediately found it to be significantly more effective than conventional open water configurations.

Can I Still Dive DIR While Using a Short Hose on my primary Regulator?

Technical divers nearly always use a five to seven foot hose (1.5-2 m) on the regulator they will pass to an out-of-air diver. This longer hose allows them substantially more room to manage out of air emergencies, especially in confined areas. Technical DIR divers always breathe this long hose and, in an emergency, pass it to out-of-air divers. In contrast, recreational DIR divers do not need a long hose; nonetheless, in an out-of-air emergency, they will still pass the shorter hose regulator from their mouth. Even so, the longer emergency hose can still be very beneficial for air sharing in the open water as it allows for a very comfortable length of hose to be deployed. Instead of struggling with an awkward 36-inch octopus hose, divers have plenty of additional space in which to maneuver.

Though the next chapter takes up the DIR system and its application to the open water in more detail, suffice it to say here that most experienced open water DIR divers prefer to use one configuration for all the diving they might reasonably be expected to do, rather than having to alternate between different configurations for different types of diving. For example, DIR recreational divers often breathe from a longer hose and utilize a dual orifice valve on their single tank; this way they have maximum redundancy and with proper training can pursue a range of options during a particular dive. For example, if they had overhead training, they could comfortably explore coral overhangs or venture briefly into a wreck's superstructure (with proper guideline reels). Individuals that confine their diving to very shallow open water areas will likely find that the short hose regulator easily supports their diving, while those seeking to get the most out of every diving experience invariably configure themselves accordingly.

Minimalism and the Streamlined Diver

All divers should "streamline" their equipment to reduce drag and to increase efficiency. Items should not be hanging free or protruding from the diver's body as they increase drag and the risk of entanglement. In the open water, these entanglements may result from fishing line, cable, rope or coral. In an overhead, dangling items are likely to catch in the guideline or drag along mud-covered bottoms, disturbing visibility. Regardless of the environment, a streamlined diver is safer and more efficient.

The DIR system's clean configuration is well-suited to silty environments and places where entanglement poses a hazard.

©GUE, Kea, Greece

Nonetheless, dedication to the concept of streamlining varies greatly from diver to diver. Many divers who believe that they and their equipment are streamlined allow reserve lights or other gear to swing freely from their tanks. This, as we discussed earlier, is not a particularly efficient way of moving through the water. To maximize efficiency, reduce drag and minimize the risk of entanglement, all equipment must be properly positioned and secured; in other words, hoses should not only be configured to reduce entanglement, but also to simplify access to the valves.

In general, divers need to be conscious of the whole package and of the synergistic interplay of the various elements that form it; they should not favor, to the exclusion of the others, any of the elements of the system. Equipment should form a cohesive unit, one that facilitates dives; it should not be a haphazard collection of available items. More equipment is not always better, and the best approach to a dive is to bring only what is needed. Nonetheless, this rule does not preclude the use of any items relevant to a dive. For example, GUE exploration divers use the clean, DIR concept of minimalism in all forms of diving they undertake. From extensive video and still photography sessions, to aquatic research initiatives and long-range explorations, these divers are forced to make choices about what equipment will facilitate the mission and what will be better left at home. In short, minimalism and streamlining do not limit the dive. On the contrary, they allow divers the greatest comfort and flexibility to accomplish whatever they desire on any given dive. From leading edge exploration to having fun on a coral reef, divers who practice the DIR system find themselves in a position to enjoy the dive rather than struggle against their equipment.

©Jarrod Jablonski

©Wes Sadler

The DIR configuration moves smoothly from open water to an overhead environment.

Top: Deep reef exploration, Bimini, Bahamas;

Bottom: Cave 1 Training, High Springs, FL

The advantages of DIR gear configuration equally benefit the beginning open water diver and the advanced technical diver;
©Ron De Amorim, Ft. Lauderdale

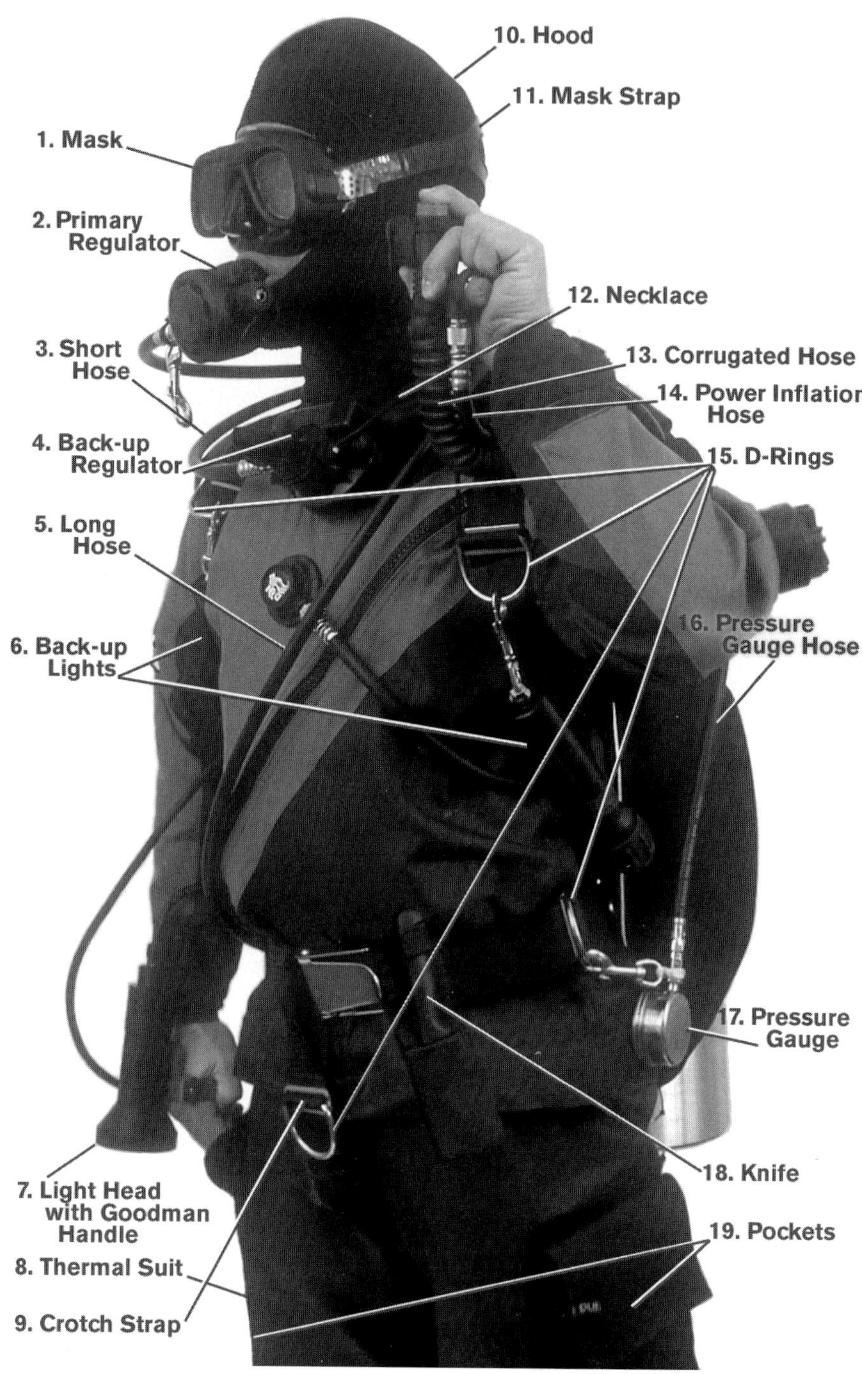

DIR Gear Configuration, Front View/Double Cylinder

Chapter 6

The Doing It Right Equipment Configuration

A good SCUBA equipment configuration needs to carry through all diving; it should allow for the addition of items necessary to perform a specific dive (e.g., an ice dive, a cave dive or an open water dive) without interfering with or changing the existing configuration. Diving with the same configuration allows for the identical response to emergencies while reducing effective task loading due to familiarity. In other words, it not only helps solve problems, it prevents them.

Following is a list of equipment as pictured on the previous page:

1. **Mask:** Low Volume mask reduces drag and requires less effort to clear it of water.
2. **Primary Regulator:** Quality regulator that will be passed to an out-of-air diver.
3. **Short Hose:** Should be long enough to breathe comfortably, but not long enough to bow and create drag.
4. **Back-Up Regulator:** Quality regulator that a diver will use as a reserve either in the event of a failure or in an air-sharing episode.
5. **Long Hose:** Optional in shallow, open water diving, but mandatory in deeper or overhead diving; the long hose simplifies air sharing. When used, the long hose, along with the primary regulator, should ALWAYS be placed on the diver's right post.
6. **Back-Up Lights:** Tucked away to reduce drag but still allow for easy one-hand removal.
7. **Goodman Handle Light Head:** Allows for hands-free diving while allowing the diver to easily direct the focused light beam.
8. **Thermal Suit:** Appropriate to keep diver alert and comfortable.
9. **Crotch Strap:** Allows for custom fit, and supports two D-rings: one works as a scooter attachment point; (divers should not hang equipment here as it would hang too low); and one further up, closer to the back plate, which works for towing additional gear. The crotch strap also holds the BC in position and prevents the BC from floating up away from the body.
10. **Hood:** Where necessary to keep diver alert and comfortable.
11. **Mask Strap:** Strong strap that will resist breaking.
12. **Necklace:** Designed to hold the back-up regulator within easy access.

13. **Corrugated Hose:** Should be just long enough to allow for ear clearing and potential dry suit inflation while actuating inflator, but not so long that it drags or entangles easily.
14. **Power Inflation Hose:** Should be long enough for a diver to easily use his/her corrugated hose, but not long enough for it to bow or otherwise create excess drag.
15. **D-rings:** No more than two on the chest, positioned to reduce the drag of attached items; one hip D-ring to hold the pressure gauge.
16. **Pressure Gauge Hose:** Custom hose allows a diver to easily read the gauge after unclipping, but does not bow or dangle, thus avoiding excess drag.
17. **Pressure Gauge:** Quality brass gauge should be easy to read and reliable.
18. **Knife:** Waist-mounted in front, near the center of the diver's body, for easy access.
19. **Pockets:** Hip-mounted to reduce drag; these pockets are ideal for storing slates, decompression tables, small guideline spools or other necessary equipment.

The following additional configuration items appear on the next two pages:

20. **Knobs:** Soft knobs (to limit risk of breakage) should be opened completely.
21. **Valve:** Contingent on environment and diving activity. Dual orifice valves (H or Manifold) are an excellent way to increase safety and redundancy.
22. **Burst Disks:** Use of double disks prevents accidental burst failure.
23. **Buoyancy Compensator:** Adjusted based upon needed lift whether one is diving single or double tanks. Buoyancy should be sufficient to float equipment by itself while at the surface.
24. **Cylinders:** Contingent on environment and diving activity.
25. **Harness and Backplate:** Designed to hold the diver snugly to their rig while reducing drag and increasing control.
26. **Primary Light:** Hip-mounted, canister-style light; this is optional in some environments, but valuable in nearly all.
27. **Alternate Lift Device:** Lift bag, diver alert marker, or surface life raft, for open water diving. Halcyon's MC system allows for storage in backplate pack for increased streamlining.
28. **Overboard Discharge:** Also known as a P-Valve; used with a

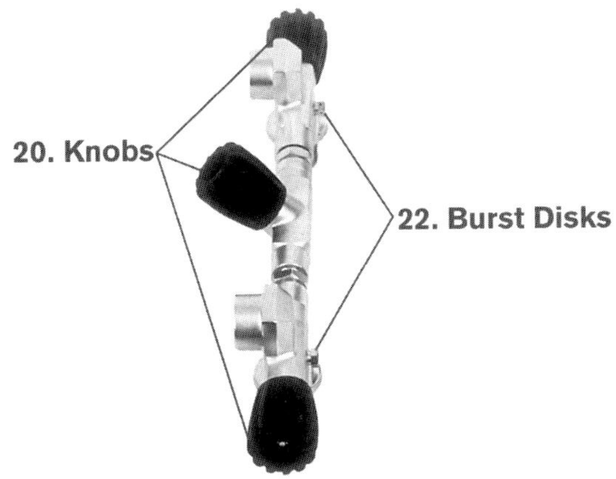

DIR Gear Configuration, Front View

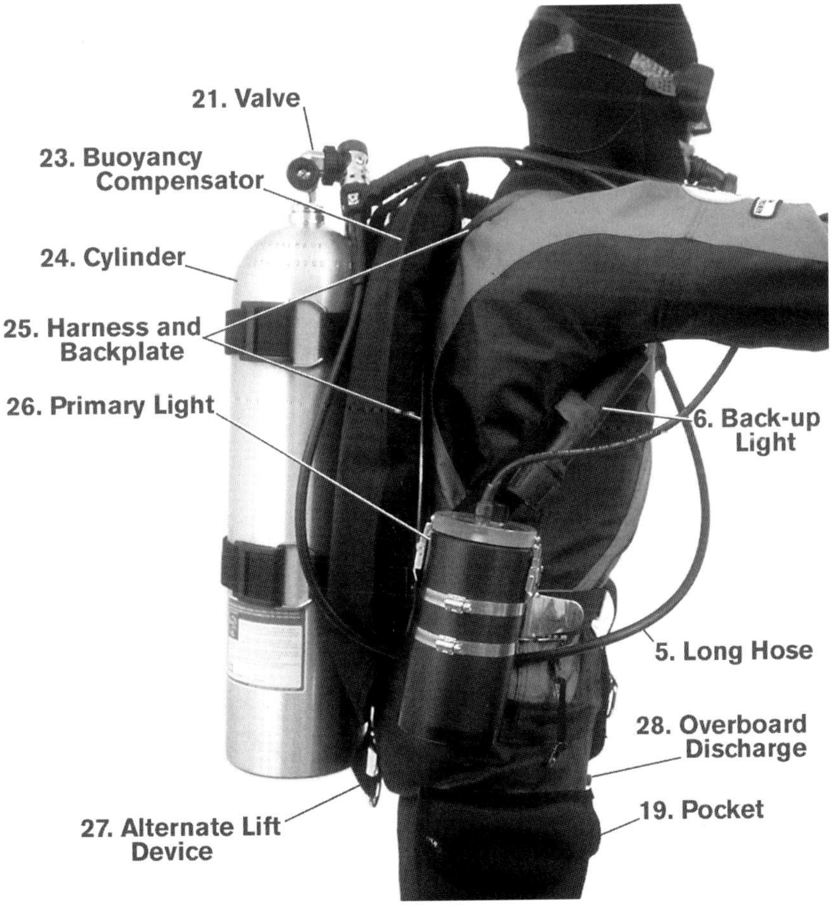

DIR Gear Configuration, Side View/Single Cylinder

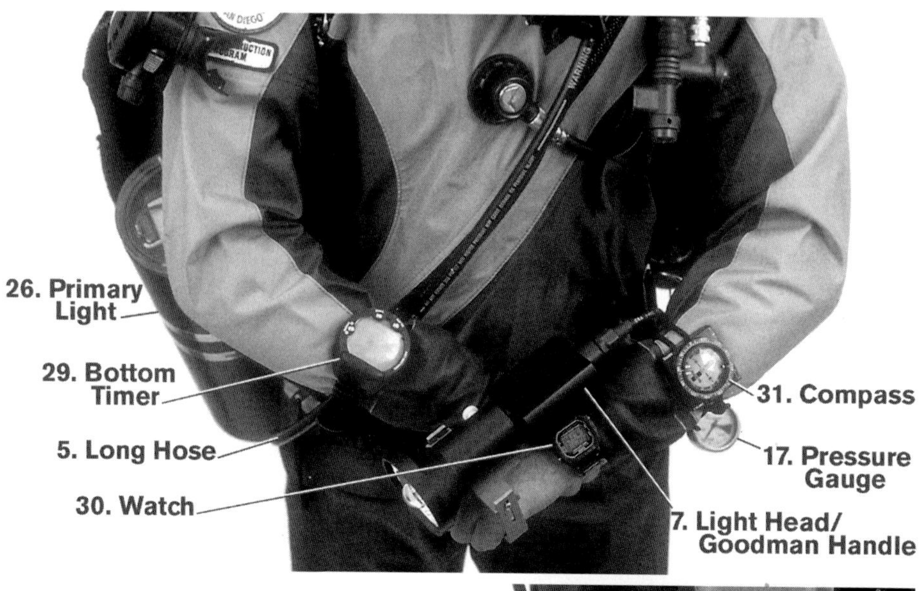

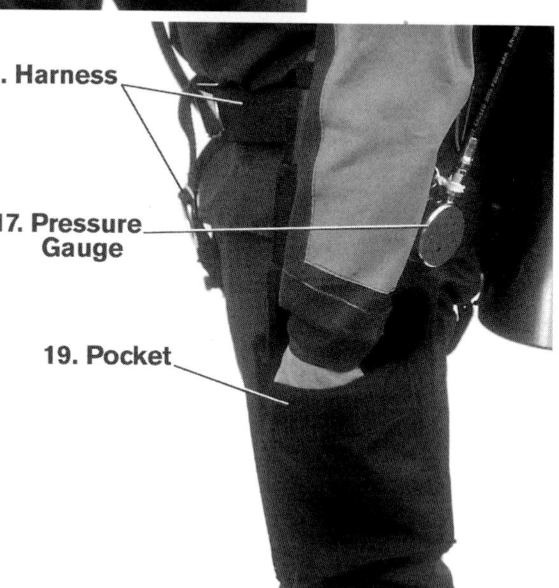

Top: DIR location of bottom timer, compass and depth gauge.
Right: The bellows pocket is located on the left leg of the exposure suit.
Bottom Left: Fins showing replacement spring-style straps.
Bottom Right: Goodman handle light head and guideline reel.

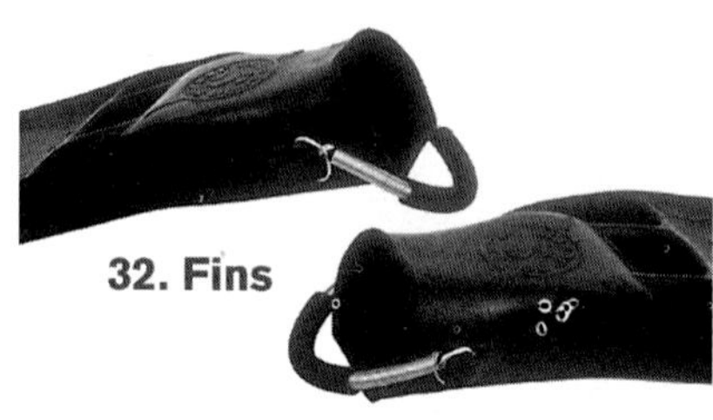

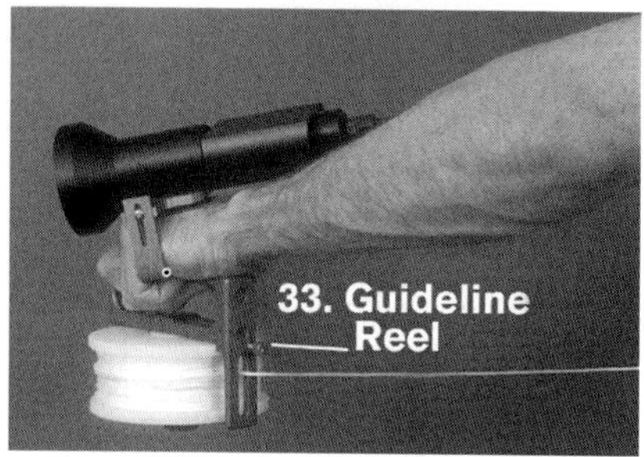

condom cathater by male divers to allow for urination during long dives with a dry suit.

29. **Bottom Timer:** Wrist mounted to eliminate drag and entanglement.
30. **Watch:** Wrist-mounted, with a functional stopwatch to allow for timing safety or decompression stops.
31. **Compass:** Wrist mounted to eliminate drag and entanglement.
32. **Fins:** These should have no attachment buckles which can break. Replace with a more robust connection.
33. **Guideline Reel:** Use is contingent on the diving environment; it is usually mounted on the rear crotch strap D-ring for streamlining and to reduce clutter. Spools and other guideline devices are usually kept in the diver's hip-mounted pocket.

DIR Details

DIR equipment configurations are almost identical across a wide range of diving environments. To adjust for specific environments, DIR divers merely add appropriate safety equipment to their DIR foundation. For example, cold water requires warmer suits and possibly gloves, while overhead diving requires additional lights (one primary and two reserve). Divers in shallow open water conditions would use smaller wings and a single tank.

The following discussion addresses the DIR system as it applies mainly to a dual regulator system. This will allow readers to see the DIR

Proper DIR regulator configuration: primary regulator from the long hose, back-up regulator is held by an elastic necklace around the neck.

equipment configuration at its most complex; nonetheless, we will make parenthetical notations with respect to more recreational configurations.

The primary regulator is breathed during normal diving and passed to a diver in the event of an air-sharing emergency. When used, this regulator is usually affixed to a long hose, which in an air-sharing emergency allows the out-of-air diver additional length and comfort. Technical dives, e.g., overhead dives or deep dives, *require* the use of a long hose to facilitate air sharing. The long hose is not required for shallow open water diving, but does provide several advantages for experienced divers.

In the event of a primary regulator failure or out-of-air emergency, the backup regulator must be instantly accessible. Too often, divers leave this valuable piece of equipment hanging free or tucked away in a pocket. DIR divers hang this regulator around the neck where it can always be found and is immediately accessible. This regulator is held in place by a necklace made from elastic tubing or cord, often with a wire tie affixing it to the mouthpiece. Furthermore, having this regulator placed close to the neck means that it is less likely to be affected by surrounding water turbulence (causing a free flow). The elastic cord also provides a strap to hold that regulator tightly in the mouth when necessary.[1] The backup regulator should be a non-air-balanced, lower

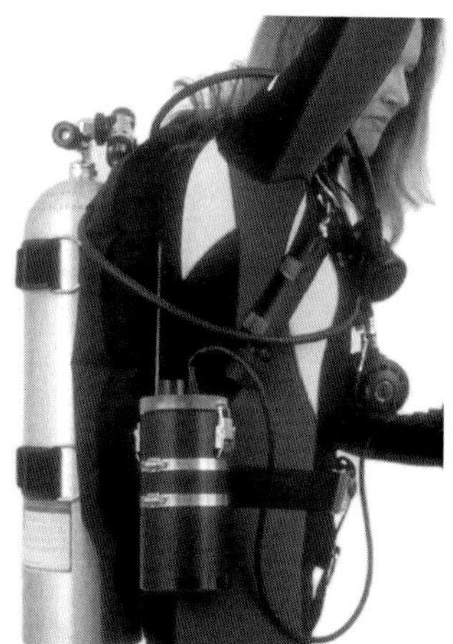

Correct routing of the 5ft. long hose under the diver's right arm and around the neck. The backplate/harness system is streamlined and comfortable for all diving applications.

[1] **Advanced Technical Diver Note:** Holding the regulator in place with this strap can be beneficial in the event that a diver is suspected of an unconscious or toxic event, such as one associated with symptoms of oxygen toxicity. Divers using hyperoxic mixes would then need to switch to a gas with the lowest oxygen content; this should nearly always be in the tanks on one's back.

performance regulator that will be less likely to free flow uncontrollably. For example, a diver may use a high performance first stage for his/her primary, but should consider a less sensitive a backup regulator.

Wearing a SCUBA Tank

Historically, divers believed that diving with a harness and a back-mounted wing was only suitable for double tank technical diving. However, divers have now come to realize that a back-mounted "wing-style" BC (adjusted for the amount of lift required) is a better overall choice for a diver, providing him/her with an array of advantages not possible with conventional jacket-style units. This is because a classic style open water BC is not only necessarily bulky and loose fitting, it also tends to force a diver's feet into a downward angle, a terrible swimming position, thereby increasing drag and effort.

Most technical divers recognize the inferiority of a jacket-style BC for use with double tanks; nonetheless, they often do not fully appreciate how many of these same problems plague open water divers. For example, conventional jacket-style BCs try to fit a wide range of divers with only a handful of stock sizes. Consequently, for most, they do not provide a snug fit and result in increased drag, greater discomfort and tanks rolling from side to side. Tank movement is uncomfortable; it pulls a diver from one side to another, and as a consequence not only limits his/her efficiency, but also makes his/her precision buoyancy control much more difficult. Lastly, the additional drag associated with a jacket BC translates directly into more work for the diver, and therefore into more stress and less fun.

In contrast to sloppy fitting jacket-style BCs, harness systems fit all divers snugly and with great precision, and are infinitely adjustable. When fitted with an appropriately sized wing-style compensator, these systems provide the absolute best combination of streamlining and comfort. Since streamlining and comfort are equally important for both open water and technical divers, it is no wonder that many manufacturers, trying to cash in on the popularity of technical diving, have tried to mimic the benefits of this harness system by constructing hybrid versions. In some cases, these systems are improvements on the traditional jacket-style BCs; nonetheless, they never manage to match the precision fit or the streamlining of a harness system.

The Harness and Backplate

A diver's harness should be rigged from one piece of webbing and should have no quick-release buckles or other failure points. Though plastic quick-release buckles seem to simplify the process of getting into and out of one's dive gear, these "savings" are illusory. Rather than save time, these devices can actually put a diver at greater risk than s/he would be without it. For example, quick-release buckles can fail during a dive and, as a consequence, a diver's life support equipment can pull away from him/her during a critical moment in the dive. Individuals that understand climbing, parachuting or other harness-dependent activities should naturally be sceptical about the "savings" found in anything that allows their equipment to "easily come off." Most seasoned divers cringe at the thought of losing the tanks from their backs.

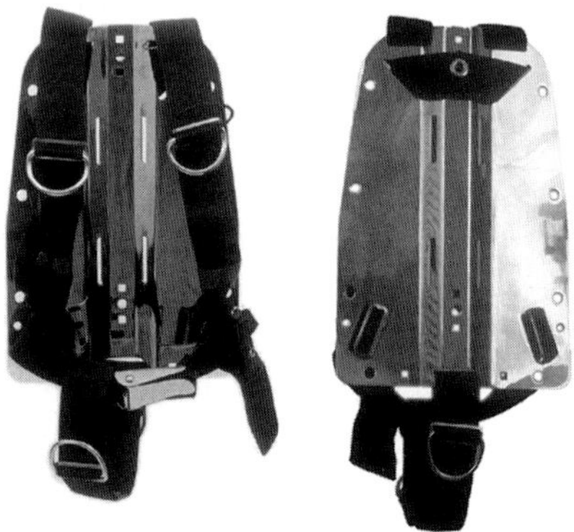

Front and back views of a steel backplate. The harness is rigged from a single piece of webbing.

In many cases this could prove fatal as the diver clings to tanks whose negative tendency stands in stark contrast to his/her own positive tendency.

The crotch strap is also one piece, and has a loop in the front through which the waist belt is threaded. The crotch strap is needed to hold the diving system in place and to prevent it from sliding up towards the head when entering the water or when inverting; later it will also be necessary for any diving involving a diver propulsion vehicle (DPV). Once threaded through the crotch strap, the belt buckle should be placed to the right of center so as not to get accidentally opened by the crotch strap.[2]

Furthermore, the area below the tanks is an excellent area for storing equipment. A D-ring attached high on the crotch strap provides ample room for storing items like reels, lift bags and reserve scooters. In addi-

[2] Chest straps or poorly fitting equipment, which shifts when the diver moves or inverts, markedly increases a diver's breathing rate and discomfort because it puts upward pressure on the diaphragm.

tion, this D-ring also provides a diver experiencing a DPV failure with a handhold, enabling them to be towed out quickly and efficiently by another DPV diver. The efficiency of this system and the time it saves is remarkable.

Commonly, manufacturers adorn their harnesses with several poorly placed D-rings, often incorrectly shaped and of poor design. In contrast, the DIR harness is the model of simplicity. To avoid the unnecessary clutter of multiple attachments, the DIR harness only supports one D-ring on each side of the chest, one D-ring on the diver's left hip and two D-rings on the crotch strap. The chest D-rings should be bent slightly so that only one hand is needed to clip bottles to them. The hip D-ring is used for pressure gauges, stage bottles, and other gear, while the crotch strap D-rings are used for DPV attachment (front) and towing (see above). Individuals should not clip equipment to the front D-ring, because it will hang too low and will create entanglements and drag; divers should clip off any additional gear that is being towed to the rear crotch strap D-ring. Divers carrying dozens of bottles, multiple scooters and cameras manage very effectively with only these D-rings. Equipment management involves good technique, not quantity of D-rings.

The knife is placed in an open sheath on the waist belt where either hand can quickly deploy it; it should be located to the left of the crotch strap. The knife is small and is designed as a line-cutting tool.

Two back-up lights are attached to each of the two chest D-rings, one light per side. Each is held to the strap by an elastic band. This puts them beneath a diver's shoulders, where they are completely accessible but out of the way. Divers can always reach these lights and turn them on without unclipping them from their D-rings. Turning on a back up light before unclipping it is very important; divers could easily drop their back-up light while trying to get it unclipped before turning it on. This is a common disadvantage of other storage locations. [3]

When diving a single tank, this harness system can be mounted to the cylinder using a single tank adaptor; the BC would then sit between the plate and the single tank.[4] When diving double cylinders, the back-

[3] Back-up lights placed in pockets or on tanks are not easily deployed and may activate without the diver's knowledge. Such scenarios will drain the batteries over the course of one or multiple dives, leaving the light useless when most needed.

The single tank adaptor allows the diver to mount a single tank to a backplate/harness system.

plate is bolted to the cylinders with a buoyancy wing sandwiched in-between the two. In either case, the amount of wing-lift (i.e., size of wing) each diver chooses will largely depend on the kind of diving they are doing.

Backplates are generally constructed of aluminum or stainless steel. Steel backplates should be used when additional weight is required to offset the positive buoyancy of a particular exposure suit/tank combination, such as a drysuit and positive tanks.

Buoyancy Compensators

Many divers mistakenly believe that they must have large buoyancy compensators to support their diving needs. Actually, divers do not need excessive amounts of lift; large wings, because of the additional material they require, only serve to increase drag. However, if, in fact, a diver does need more than 65 pounds of lift for diving doubles, or more than 30 pounds for diving singles, then they do not have a balanced rig and are an accident waiting to happen.[5] The diver should be able to drop unnecessary weight and swim up without a functioning BC. Use of large steel cylinders indicates an aggressive dive, one that should only be done in a dry suit, which provides not only good insulation but also additional lift. As with all diving, the key component to proper buoyancy is diving with a properly balanced rig.

Divers using dual BCs have experienced an array of problems; these include increased drag, additional task loading and uncontrolled inflation. There is never a need for "redundant buoyancy" in a properly

[4] The Halcyon backplate and wing system is unique in its ability to accept single tanks without a single tank adaptor. This allows divers even greater streamlining and efficiency.

[5] Cf. section on cylinders.

balanced rig. A small leak from the inflator can continually add air to an unaware diver's BC. As the diver becomes more positive, s/he will usually try to empty his/her primary BC, all the while remaining unaware of the secondary inflation. If the diver is unable to correct this problem quickly enough, s/he may find her/himself at the surface experiencing any number of problems. The DIR approach avoids the use of dual BCs, and instead stresses proper balance between BC, cylinders, weighting and exposure suit.

Some BC's have become known as "bondage wings" because they support a series of elastic bands that restrict the size of the wings. When the BC wing is inflated, the bands are supposed to stretch so that the wings can fully inflate; in turn, when the wing is deflated, the bands are

Left: The Halcyon wing is streamlined and specifically designed for DIR. Right: The excess fabric of the "bondage wing" BC creates a whole range of unnecessary problems, including uneven inflation and increased drag.

supposed to pull down the wing's excess material. This design introduces a whole new range of problems for the diver who selects to use them. These include: uneven inflation and, as a result, off-kilter trim, the potential exacerbation of small BC punctures as a result of the bungee squeezing air from the BC, increased drag because of the turbulence caused by an uneven surface, and, lastly, resistance to manual inflation. In short, bondage style wings have no place in DIR diving configurations.

Historically, divers have had to make a number of changes to their BC in order to increase its reliability. In many cases, these changes are still prudent, particularly if the manufacturer does not understand or appreciate the DIR system. The DIR diver can make some fairly simple changes to these wings to increase their ease of operation and to extend their longevity. First, if the wing is not constructed with internal protection for the bladder, then the inner bladder can be covered with inner tube material to protect it against being punctured. Second, the corrugated hose on nearly all BCs is far too long and therefore, because of its length, often impossible to streamline. By refitting the BC with a shorter corrugated hose, and coupling it with a custom inflator hose, the diver can significantly improve the cleanliness of his/her system. Finally, all BC fittings should be checked to ensure that they are secure. Alternatively, divers can avoid all these modifications, and purchase a BC that is specifically designed for DIR, namely, the Halcyon BC.

Regulators

By not being as subject to weather as are other sports, scuba diving can be taken up in a variety of environments and conditions. Though this is one of diving's most fascinating features, it is also what places great demands on equipment. A deep wreck dive in the frigid waters of the Baltic Sea makes different demands on a regulator than does a shallow cave dive in the fresh, warm, waters of the Yucatan. This means that, before evaluating a regulator's performance, divers should consider how and where a regulator will be used. This important, but often overlooked, step will ensure that the regulator chosen suits its intended use.

Right: DIN first stage
Left: Yoke first stage.

Regulators may be divided by use as follows:

- *Primary regulator:* worn on the diver's back and breathed during normal diving
- *Back up regulator:* worn on a diver's back but not breathed

(backup)
- *Decompression regulator:* used on a decompression bottle
- *Stage regulator:* used on stages typically at depth and to extend bottom time
- *Argon regulator:* used for suit inflation

Many divers prefer a high-performance, balanced, second stage as their primary regulator, and a slightly lower performance, unbalanced, second stage as their backup.[6] With respect to performance and reliability, this proven configuration gives a diver the best of both worlds. The balanced regulator offers maximum performance and ease of breathing, while the unbalanced regulator offers the added security of knowing that one has a safe and reliable backup. Stage bottle regulators are used to extend bottom time; so many divers prefer to use a similar regulator to that used as a primary. However, stage and deco first stages are more likely to be flooded with water, making piston-style regulators a common favorite.[7] Argon bottle regulators should be robust in design and function well at a low intermediate pressure.

Two areas that tend to generate confusion are a regulator's breathing performance and its first stage intermediate pressure. The intermediate pressure (INP) is the internal pressure in the regulator's first stage. Generally speaking, the higher this pressure is, the more force is available to deliver air to the diver. However, elevated INP also increases wear on internal components, most notably on the high pressure seat which regulates air flow as it rests against or moves away from the orifice. Most regulators have an INP of approximately 140 psi. However, some regu-

---

[6] High performance regulators used as backups are likely to free flow and cause a loss of gas supply.

[7] **Advanced Technical Diver Note:** Typically, water is not able to enter a regulator, because air pressure in the first stage holds out ambient water. However, when the tank valve is closed, the air in the regulator's first stage can be depleted by accidentally or intentionally pressing the second stage purge button. Purging the system, while the air is off, can lead to water being introduced into the regulator. Since, to prevent the accidental loss of a cylinder's contents, stage and decompression regulators must be turned off when not in use, they are more likely to be flooded by ambient water. Most regulators are tolerant of being flooded in this fashion, but most piston-style regulators are especially durable in these conditions. Furthermore, because technical divers who have a regulator failure on one decompression cylinder will usually transfer another working stage regulator onto this bottle to utilize the contents, these regulators may be intentionally flooded. While this is possible with most regulators, piston regulators are less likely to develop problems as a result.

lators are designed to run at a higher internal pressure (e.g., some regulators from the Poseidon line); these are not recommended. Most regulators deliver enough air to exceed the demand of most divers. At depths below 100' (30m), where the density of air would introduce breathing resistance problems, divers switch to Helium based mixes, which at 300' (90m) are similar to breathing air at the surface.

There are two basic types of regulator first stages: piston and diaphragm. A piston regulator is available either balanced or unbalanced (often referred to as "standard"). Unbalanced or "standard" piston first stages should only be considered for shallow low-demand applications. The balanced-piston first stage allows massive quantities of air to flow through a large piston, and is considered an extremely high performer. One of the most popular models of balanced-piston regulators will drain an eighty cubic foot cylinder in less than a minute (more than what a diver can breathe). On the other hand, a balanced-diaphragm regulator, because of the small size and low mass of its internal mechanism, can respond quickly to inhalation demands, and so may be perceived by the diver as more sensitive.

Another important consideration in choosing a regulator is the water temperature in which the regulator will be used. Not all regulators are adequate for the extremes of ice and arctic diving. Generally, diaphragm regulators are more reliable in water that is colder than 40° F (4° C) because their sealed mechanisms resist freezing. Nonetheless, several manufacturers offer cold-water kits for their piston regulators that help prevent water from entering and ice from jamming the mechanism in a free-flowing position. The best recommendation for cold-water divers, who dive in arctic conditions at least half the time, is that they use a diaphragm regulator, and consider a piston regulator with a cold-water kit only for occasional use.

Second Stage

Regulator second stages are also available in balanced and unbalanced forms. Practically, what differentiates a balanced from unbalanced second stage is that the former is a better performer while the latter is trouble-free and more reliable. The balanced second stage is depth compensated, which means that it will breathe the same at any depth. The tradeoff, however, is that in order to increase performance, one also increases complexity. This entails that the balanced second stage is more susceptible to problems, e.g., slight leaking, which, on some models, may require constant attention.[8] Total failure is uncommon with any regulator. On the other hand, though the unbalanced second stage does not give optimal performance, its simple design increases the likelihood of trouble-free operation.

Some second stages have an adjustment knob that, by moving the regulator seat closer to the orifice (see picture/diagram), allows the diver to increase or decrease regulator sensitivity. Higher performance regulators typically have this second stage adjustment; this should never be completely turned down because it will indent the seating surface. Many second stages also have a switch, called a venturi adjustment, which facilitates air delivery by adjusting a flow vane in the second stage body. Depending on its setting, this flow vane can either impede the flow of breathing gas to the diver's mouth (reducing the likelihood of free flow) or direct greater volumes to it. Lastly, several companies have second stages with storage mechanisms that are designed to hold the seating sur-

Top: Non-adjustable second stage.
Bottom: Adjustable second stage.

[8] **Advanced Technical Diver Note:** In addition to being balanced or unbalanced, second stage regulators can also be classified as upstream or downstream. Upstream regulators have a seating mechanism that sits upstream of the orifice. Should this mechanism fail, the seat would be pushed closed against the orifice, preventing air from escaping at the second stage. Upstream designs require a custom second stage hose with an integrated over-pressure relief, so that the hose does not explode from the increasing internal pressure. Such hoses are expensive, non-standard, more complex, and ill-advised. The Poseidon *Odin* is an example of the few upstream regulators currently on the market. In contrast, most second stages have downstream valves; failure will cause air to flow uncontrollably from them. Regulators that require custom hoses should be avoided. All second stages should be of the downstream-type.

face away from the orifice; this occurs during storage, when seats typically rest against the orifices and can become indented. When pressurized, the seats will then allow air to pass. However, this type of problem is more indicative of a regulator that is rarely used, and "storage devices" are not without their problems, occasionally creating free flow or performance issues if left in place or accidentally engaged.

Hoses

Divers should use high quality hoses, thereby reducing the risk of hose rupture.[9] Most importantly, hoses should be replaced every several years or when they begin to show wear. All hoses should be fitted with strain relief to reduce the risk of kinking and failure. While under pressure, divers should periodically pull the protector aside to ensure that there are no leaks or impending failures.

Long hoses typically range from 5 to 7' (1.5- 2m). Shallow open water divers who do not use a long hose commonly use a standard 32" (12.6cm) hose.

Overhead divers should use a 7' hose. Open water divers who use a long hose often use a 5 or 6' hose, depending on their size and the use of a hip-mounted canister.[10]

Deploying the 5' hose.

[9] Divers should be careful to avoid hoses that are especially buoyant or prone to wear.

[10] In open water areas where the long hose is not mandatory, short stature divers sometimes prefer to reduce the length of a long hose to five or six feet. On most divers the five foot hose does not require the diver to tuck excess hose under a light canister or in the belt. However, most DIR divers prefer to use a seven foot hose tucked under the light canister on all dives.

Deploying the 7' hose.

Restrictive areas, like caves, often require that divers travel single file. This means that unless divers are equipped with a long hose second stage, in the event of a failure, they will be unable to effectively share air in such an environment. The use of the long hose was primarily designed to manage air-sharing problems in restrictive areas, and has been a standard feature of cave diving for many years. In time, divers realized that the long hose offered advantages to anyone who might have to manage an air-sharing situation. Anytime divers are forced to travel (either swimming or scootering) while air sharing, using the long hose is mandatory. Furthermore, divers facing decompression, who are diving on or in a wreck, or who are diving in areas where a direct ascent is not feasible, will use a long hose. Today, many open water divers also choose to integrate the use of the long hose into their diving because of the additional comfort it provides during air-sharing situations. Divers that are both properly trained and equipped (lights, reels, etc.) often dive with a long hose; this allows them greater flexibility while diving (e.g., to venture into an overhead area). Due to the way it rests against the body, the long hose is also more comfortable, particularly while scootering, where its placement reduces the drag and cavitation one would experience from a shorter hose.

The backup regulator hose should come across the diver's shoulder, allowing the regulator to sit below the chin without the hose bulging to the side.

Diving in a shallow, open water environment allows a diver direct ascent to the surface, thereby reducing air-sharing complications. In this case, divers will sometimes use shorter primary regulator hoses, an acceptable practice in this environment. Divers will not have to travel any distance while air sharing, as they should be able to manage an urgent situation using an emergency swimming ascent where a breath hold is sufficient to reach the surface.[11] Obviously, such an event is only for emergencies. Divers ascending from SCUBA on a breath-hold must exhale during the ascent to prevent embolism. This technique should be practised and discussed during open water training; but air sharing-techniques and good buddy skills should always be emphasized over emergency breath-hold ascents. [12]

Power inflator hoses should run over the diver's left shoulder and be long enough to comfortably supply the power inflator, while not so long that they bulge out to either side. In turn, the inflator itself should be long enough that, with one hand controlling all manoeuvres, a diver is able to easily reach his/her mouth, his/her dry suit inflation valve, and his/her nose; it should also be long enough that, if necessary, one could

Side and front views of DIR hose routing on a single tank system.

[11] Breath-hold ascents occasionally result from equipment problems, but are almost always the result of careless diving habits where divers ignore their gas supply. Even out-of-air emergencies only result in breath-hold ascents when divers fail to adhere to the buddy system.

[12] Many people find that the longer hose primary not only facilitates air sharing, but also greatly simplifies low-on-gas situations. In these situations a diver with ample gas supply can pass the long hose to a diver low on gas while the team makes a comfortable return to the boat and/or surface. Instructors and dive leaders often find this flexibility extremely helpful.

DIR hose routing on a double tank system. The primary regulator hose and BC inflator hose are always run from the diver's right post. The back-up regulator hose, the SPG hose, and the drysuit inflator hose are run from the diver's left post.

breathe out of it by simultaneously holding down both buttons.[13] The inflator from the wings runs over the shoulder and through a small bungie attached with the left chest D-ring. This keeps the inflator where it can be located instantly. Simply put, the hose should run smoothly from the diver's right regulator post, behind the neck and to the power inflator.

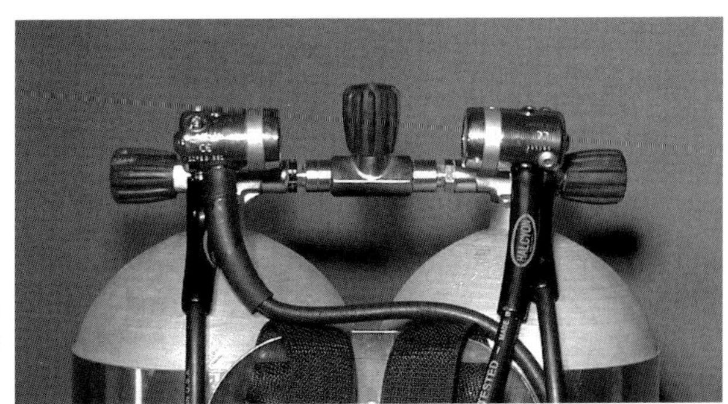

Close up view of hoses coming off the right and left posts.

[13] **Advanced Technical Diver Note:** It is possible to breathe from a power inflator. This note does not recommend that one do so, only that as a last resort it offers an alternative to drowning. In such an event, divers should push the power inflator button while depressing the inflator exhaust and breathe from the mouthpiece. One must breathe from the fresh gas supply, not re-breathe gas in the corrugated hose, and then exhale into the water. Improper technique will result in unconsciousness; so it is not an option on which one should embark casually.

To provide additional redundancy when using two first stages, the inflator hose should always be run from the right post. This requirement is illustrated in the case of a diver's left post rolling off or breaking. If the inflator is run from the left post, the diver will simultaneously lose not only the use of the backup regulator around the neck but also the ability to inflate the BC. These two problems together could be inordinately compounded by an out-of-air situation in which a diver would not only be without the means of controlling his/her buoyancy but would also be deprived of the use of a third regulator (cf. note 7). In addition, the inflator mechanism itself should not be designed to fill rapidly; this allows one to manage a runaway inflation more effectively, should an inflator failure cause a continual addition of air. Rapid inflation devices are designed to compensate for poor diving skill, and in doing so actually compound diver risk; part of having good form, the hallmark of a safe diver, requires that a diver must anticipate his or her inflation needs.

The pressure gauge hose should run from the diver's left post to the left hip D-ring, where it is attached by a stainless steel clip wire-tied to the pressure gauge. This pressure gauge does not need a protective boot, nor does it need to be in a console or in any other device that increases its size and/or entanglement potential. The hose should be short enough to stay out of the slipstream and long enough to allow for viewing of the gauge once it is unclipped from the D-ring.

Left: SPG is clipped onto the left hip D-ring when not in use.
Right: The SPG hose is long enough to allow viewing when unclipped.

Regulator Configuration

Diving With One First Stage

Shallow, open water divers often use one first stage attached to a single tank. This configuration is very similar to that used by a double tank diver. With a single regulator, the two second stages come over the diver's right shoulder while the pressure gauge and power inflator run to the left. Although most experienced divers choose to use a long hose for all their diving needs, the shallow open water diver may choose not to use one.[14]

Diving With Two First Stages

Divers use double tanks for technical diving not only because they seek to increase their available air supply, but also because they understand the safety margin provided by redundancy. Therefore, the use of double tanks usually indicates deeper or overhead diving. Likewise, single tank divers who choose to dive in deeper areas or in overhead environments must also adhere to equipment redundancy, and use a "Y" or "H" valve to allow two first stages to be affixed to a single tank. Both systems require the following configuration. Open water divers using a single tank should assume that all necessary hoses run from one first stage.

Diver's right and diver's left side views of the properly configured DIR diver.

[14] In order to gain a full appreciation for how hoses are used and routed in a DIR doubles configuration, open-water divers are encouraged to read the section on diving with two first stages. The routing logic revealed there applies to all areas of diving, from open water to technical. Most individuals will appreciate the logic of this robust system.

In a doubles configuration, the primary second stage regulator is attached via a long hose to a first stage that is affixed to the diver's right post (right shoulder). This configuration not only ensures redundancy, but also facilitates gas sharing. The long hose runs straight down behind the wing, under the light canister (if one is worn, if not it is routed around the knife, or tucked into the belt), back up the left side, and around the neck; the attached second stage is then placed in one's mouth and breathed.

When not in use, e.g., during stage diving or during decompression, this regulator is clipped off to the right chest D-ring using a breakaway clip.[15] During an emergency air-sharing episode, divers will have to unclip this regulator to pass it to an out-of-air diver. While using stage or deco bottles, donors should pass the regulator in their mouth (stage or deco) and then deploy the long hose. Passing it off from the mouth assures the right gas is given to the out-of-air diver. In most cases, divers will pass the stage bottle over to the out-of-air diver and commence

Front view of the properly configured DIR divers, with O_2 bottles.

©Steve Auer

[15] **Advanced Technical Diver Note:** Breakaway clips are designed to facilitate the rapid deployment of an item that is secured to a D-ring. This is particularly beneficial for re-breather divers or those with very thick gloves, who would find unclipping a snap particularly difficult or time consuming. This is not an excuse for poor technique; most divers will not have cause to use this connection. Divers that are breathing off a stage or decompression bottle should clip the long hose second stage to their right D-ring. This prevents them from inadvertently breathing their back gas instead of their decompression/stage bottle and also keeps their long hose second stage from dragging along the bottom or becoming entangled. The breakaway clip should be strong enough that it requires a strong pull to break free. This is best accomplished with a thin cable tie or o-ring.

breathing off the long hose. Should the out-of-air diver need additional decompression gas, the divers will likely take turns using the bottle (such as five minutes each) or buddy-breathe. To reduce delay—with re-breather diving, with cold fingers and/or thick gloves—divers usually affix a breakaway section to the clip on their long hose to enable them to pull the hose free from the clip. Out-of-air divers should also be practised in going directly to the long hose, and be able to breathe from it while it is still clipped off, deploying it later without assistance. Divers must also practice quickly deploying the long hose in a variety of situations.

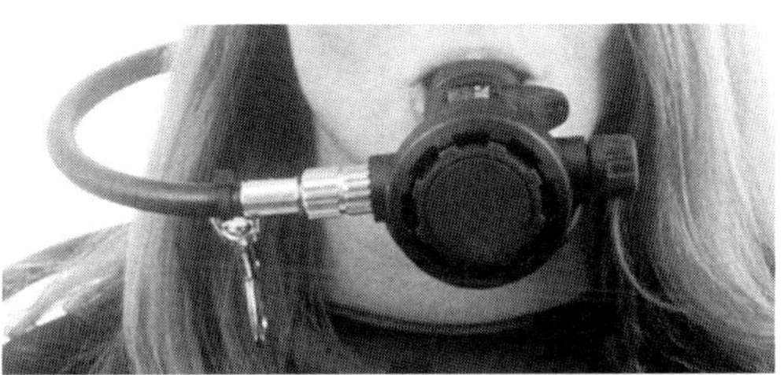

The primary regulator has a stainless steel clip so it may be clipped off to the right chest D-ring when not in use.

Divers should NEVER put their primary regulator on the left post because they risk a post roll off during contact with an overhead. Furthermore, severe contact might cause this knob to be severed in the off position, leaving the diver without a long hose in case of an emergency. Placing the long hose on the diver's right post means that the post can only be rolled open, and, in the case of a broken knob, will still be usable (both knobs turn clockwise but are on opposing sides). Furthermore, placing the long hose on the left post not only effectively shortens the hose for sharing, it also complicates proper routing; this is because it must cross an additional foot to get to the right post and to the out-of-air diver. Lastly, the oblique angles required to thread the long hose across the back can also restrict gas flow. In short, routing the hose from any other post than the right one is illogical and risky.

As with any new technique, divers that are new to managing a long hose may notice an early learning curve. However, a couple of dives should be sufficient for them to become proficient in managing a long hose. While on the surface, divers should be careful not to drop the second stage in the dirt, and drag it by the long hose behind them. Whenever it is not in use, irrespective of whether this is at depth or on the surface, divers should become habituated to clipping off their long hose to their right D-ring.

While diving, hoses generally float and sit comfortably against one's body. Since, for purposes of gas exchange and general good form a diver should always be in a supine position, this long hose will usually be held in place against the body.[16]

Does the Long Hose Decrease Regulator Performance?

Regulators can easily supply air through a long hose without registering any notable drop in breathing performance. If there is any reduction in regulator performance when using the long hose, it is negligible, and in all but the lowest performance regulators, not even a noteworthy concern. If being attached to a long hose diminishes a regulator's performance, then the regulator itself is not suitable for normal diving use. Configure the long hose to breathe to one's preference by having a technician adjust the intermediate pressure of the first stage. Higher intermediate pressures will result in better regulator performance; however, it is important to recognize that keeping the pressure moderately low helps to reduce regulator fatigue and the risk of freezing. While diving deeper than about 100' (30m), helium becomes a larger component of one's breathing mix. With helium, ease of breathing is greatly increased, thereby eliminating concerns regarding increased resistance while diving deeper.[17]

[16] An important note to make in this discussion of hoses is the underlying logic that supports the elements of the system. Every element of hose distribution and routing is analyzed in terms of overall efficiency and simplicity; all elements here are complimentary, and function holistically to empower the diver.

[17] **Advanced Technical Diver Note:** Due to the dangers associated with narcosis, increased gas density, CO_2 accumulation, and oxygen toxicity risk, air is a wholly inappropriate gas for diving much beyond 100' (30m). The density of air can initiate an insidious loop with continually elevated CO_2 accumulation exacerbating narcosis and leading to impairment, elevated risk and potential fatalities. Nitrogen is seven times denser than helium, and impacts a diver's ability to ventilate (remove CO_2); this, of course, limits his/her work capability at depth. Breathing air at the surface is similar to breathing a heliox mixture at more than 200' (60m). A wide range of gas physiology issues is thoroughly presented in GUE's technical diving manual. Realistically, any breathing performance problems are the result of very poor regulator choices or completely inappropriate diving gasses.

The streamlined diver has no dangling consoles or gauges.

Gauges

Historically, divers have been led to believe that consolidating an array of gauges into one bulky console and then dragging that console along behind them was somehow a sensible and responsible practice. Not true. By dragging a bulky console behind them, divers not only kill whatever coral with which they come in contact, they also risk significant entanglement. Instead, divers should wear their depth gauge and compass on their wrist or forearm. In this position, not only will they be immediately accessible, they will also not drag along the bottom, killing coral or risking entanglement. In the ocean, a compass is of para-

Depth gauge on the diver's right, compass and dive watch on the left.

mount importance, and, without interfering with other activities, needs to be viewable and held in its correct orientation. It should be on the left hand, away from one's scooter (if used), to avoid the motor's disruptive magnetic field. The bottom timer/depth gauge needs to be viewable at all times and should be placed on the right hand.

Mask

The mask should fit comfortably, be low volume (to reduce drag, simplify clearing, and increase vision), and be of durable construction. The lenses should not remove too easily because they may become dislodged accidentally during transport, or more seriously, during the dive itself. The strap must be secure and resilient, thereby limiting the risk of the mask being dislodged or the strap breaking. After-market straps that substitute a neoprene-style attachment for the original may be more comfortable and are nearly unbreakable.

Although long popular, high volume masks (left) don't offer any advantages over a low volume mask.

Technical divers are often in the water for hours and sometimes carry a spare mask to guard against being without a mask in the event of a mask failure. If carried, a spare mask should be as small as possible while still providing a comfortable seal. This mask should be stored in a pocket on the side of one's leg. If one carries a spare mask, it is critical to check it regularly to determine whether it is still functional; also, be aware that if one deploys a spare mask underwater, it may immediately begin to fog. To prevent this from happening, the spare mask should be cleaned regularly and pre-treated with a concentrated de-fogging agent before the dive.

Snorkel

Snorkels are useful only while divers are at the surface; during a dive they are typically in the way. In any type of overhead diving, snorkels are not only completely useless, they also pose an entanglement threat. If snorkelling, divers should choose a snorkel with a good size tube that mounts comfortably and does not offer breathing resistance. While diving, snorkels are best left on the boat. Nonetheless, rather than choosing from the array of gimmicky snorkels common to the dive industry (i.e., those with special purge outlets), divers should learn proper skin diving techniques. For example, the displacement clear makes snorkel clearing very simple.

FINS

Stiff blade fins pushed by a diver with good leg strength generate a maximum amount of thrust. Such fins are very popular among divers that require the ability to swim quickly, move against strong currents, or push large amounts of equipment through the water. Less rigid fins will work when pushing less equipment or when less power is desired. The best practice for divers is to use the same gear all the time. Divers should remove all plastic buckles from their new fins and substitute for them stronger attachment springs.

VALVES

As with most equipment, the benefits of bargain valves are questionable; therefore, divers should seek to purchase valves of long lasting quality. Common favorites are Sherwood, Beauchat, and Scubapro valves.

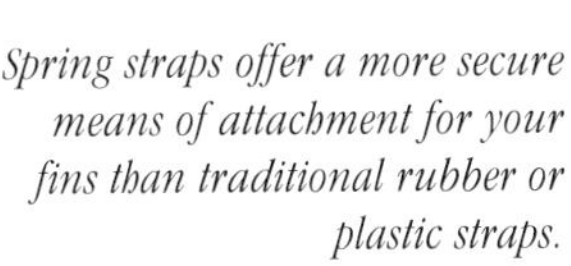

Spring straps offer a more secure means of attachment for your fins than traditional rubber or plastic straps.

Burst ports on valves and manifolds can cause serious problems should they fail. Should these release unexpectedly underwater, a diver would rapidly lose their available air supply (except in the case of an isolation manifold, which we will discuss below). To reduce this risk, technical divers typically replace these disks with higher-pressure plugs. Burst disks should be changed yearly along with the visual inspection of the cylinder.

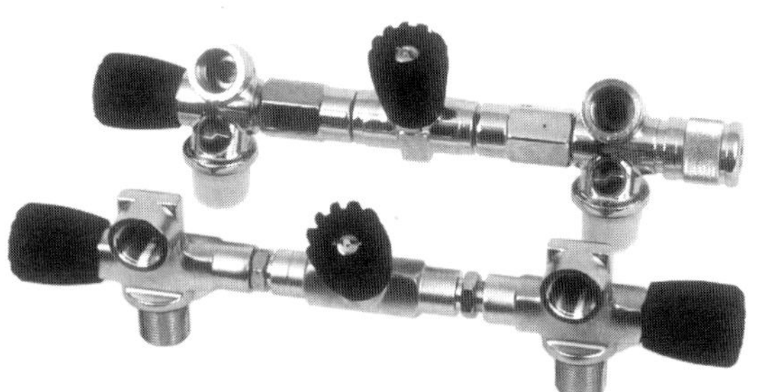

Top: Valves set at an angle increase the risk of breaking the DIN connection– and the metal knob introduces a potential failure point.
Bottom: Valves should face straight ahead.

DIN vs. Yoke

Yoke valves have been around since the advent of SCUBA diving, and are still very common around the world. Deutche International Norm (DIN) valves were intended to replace Yoke valves by offering a threaded design that was able to handle higher pressures. DIN valves are available in 200 bar (3,000 psi), and in longer threaded 300 bar (4,400 psi), a difference that reflects their respective working pressure. DIN valves also reduce problems by employing orifice o-rings; nonetheless, divers should be aware that the o-ring on the regulator end of the DIN connection tube could come loose if a diver mistakenly twists the first stage to loosen the regulator-to-tank connection. For this reason, divers should only turn the hand wheel to remove the regulator.

Knobs

Knobs should be spring-loaded and soft, with a metal insert that prevents them from being stripped. Divers should not use metal knobs because, in addition to being harder to turn efficiently, they have a tendency of locking off or on, especially when dented by impact. In contrast, rubber knobs are durable, shock absorbent, shatterproof and easy to turn. Divers should be aware that, if rubbed along an overhead, rubber knobs could turn inadvertently. To avoid a "roll off" that would interrupt the supply of gas, it is important to check one's valves after making any contact with an overhead (a wise habit to develop regardless

Hard plastic knobs break very easily and should be replaced immediately with a suitable alternative.

of the knobs used). Plastic knobs do slightly reduce the chance of a "roll off" but can be dangerous if, on impact, they shatter. Rubber knobs—like those found on the Halcyon manifold—are very robust, while softer plastic knobs—such as those found on the Scubapro manifold—also seem to resist breaking. However, hard plastic knobs break very easily and should be replaced at once.

Manifolds

Manifolds are designed to connect two cylinders together to allow divers access to either or both cylinder. Old-style single-port manifolds allowed divers to place a single first stage on the manifold and access air from both tanks. However, in the event of regulator failure, divers would lose access to their entire air supply. As divers continued to explore deep and overhead environments, it became necessary to maximize access to their gas supply. Maximum access was accomplished by attaching two first stages to one manifold, which in most models also maintains a center shut-off valve. Should the regulator, o-ring, or hose fail, the diver merely shuts down the supply to that regulator, thereby preventing any further loss of gas. Because the valve knob nearest the regulator only controls flow to that first stage, the diver, through the manifold, still has access to the gas in both cylinders.

In the very unlikely event of a catastrophic failure of the tank neck o-ring or the burst disk, the diver can close the isolator valve and interrupt the airflow to that side of the manifold, thereby protecting the gas supply in the other cylinder. In such an event, the diver should, if possible, continue to breathe from the leaking tank until it is exhausted,

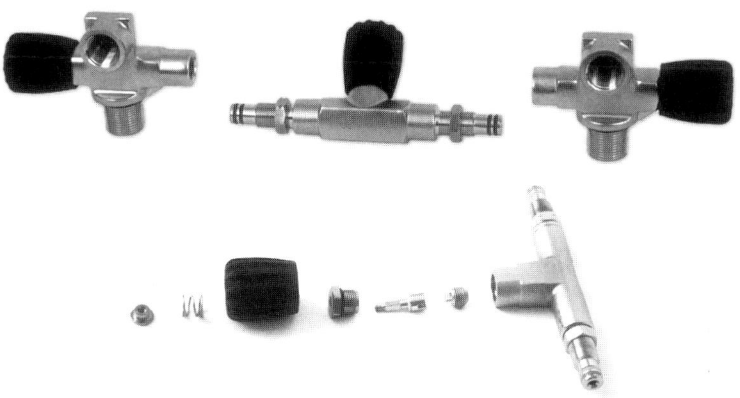

Isolator manifold: disassembled components (top) and knob assembly (bottom).

and then switch to the unused portion of the gas supply. Catastrophic scenarios aside, the most common need for an isolator stems from a broken knob where the impact also causes the manifold to leak at the valve assembly. In such a case, the leaking is usually moderate; nonetheless, by isolating the cylinders, a diver can prevent losing any of the undamaged cylinder's contents while breathing the remaining supply from the leaking cylinder.

Manifolds should have barrel-style o-rings, no face seals, and should be adjustable. The 300 bar manifold provides more threaded depth and a more secure attachment. Valves should face straight, with no angles. Manifolds that place regulators at an angle increase their exposure and elevate the risk of breaking DIN connections.

Special Note About Isolator Valves on Manifolds

One must always guard against the possibility that an isolator valve has been accidentally turned off during a fill or a safety drill; a closed isolator can create problems. The isolator should always be left completely open. Symptoms of a closed isolator depend upon which tank the diver is breathing. If the gauge and "isolated" regulator are on the same tank, the diver should notice an unusually quick depletion of his/her gas supply. Divers might mistakenly believe that they are out of gas. This is unlikely (in the DIR configuration) unless the diver has had cause to breathe from the backup regulator. If the gauge and regulator in use are on opposite sides of the isolator (as would normally be the case in DIR configurations), the gauge will continue to read the same pressure as the other tank is depleted. In this case, divers will have breathed the one tank dry and mistakenly believed that they were out of air. Realistically, this only happens to divers that are paying almost no attention to their gas supply. Unusually rapid or nonexistent depletion of gas supply is cause for evaluation and rectification.

Furthermore, if one is careless and does not check whether the isolator is open, a diver can unwittingly create a dangerous gas mix in his/her tanks. For example, during partial pressure filling, divers will first fill their tanks with pure oxygen and then top them off with air. Should the isolator be inadvertently closed after the oxygen fill, but before the air top off, one tank will be properly mixed while the other will contain pure oxygen. If, following the top off, a diver gauges one of his/her cylinders, but does not check whether the isolator is open, they stand a good chance of breathing pure oxygen at depth. This can easily be fatal. Of course, by leaving the isolator always open, by examining the isolator before and after cylinder fills, and by checking the valve immediately prior to entering the water, one can easily eliminate all of these self-induced problems.

Cylinders

The type of cylinder that a diver should choose depends on his/her diving environment and his/her other equipment. For example, most shallow open water diving requires a limited air supply, which makes aluminum 80cf cylinders nearly ideal. These tanks go from being about three pounds negative (when full) to about three pounds positive (when empty) so that the diver is not required to manage large changes in buoyancy. However, cold-water divers will usually wear dry suits with bulky undergarments, thereby increasing their positive buoyancy. To offset some of this positive buoyancy, cold-water divers add weight, in the form of either a heavier steel tank or a weighted belt.

Left: Diver wearing double cylinders. Right: Diver wearing a single cylinder.

Improper weighting, i.e., being too positive or too negative, can be very dangerous for divers. In the ocean, an over-weighted diver with buoyancy problems could find it very difficult to reach the boat, and sink ever deeper in the ocean. While in a cave, the loss of buoyancy is not as risky (because there is usually a bottom); nonetheless, divers could easily be overcome by problems associated with substantial negative weighting. Being too positive is also very dangerous. For example, ocean divers that are too positive could not stay submerged, and would risk dangerous ascents, missed decompression, or buddy separation. In an overhead environment, positive buoyancy is no less severe because, by making it nearly impossible for divers to stay off the ceiling and swim out of an overhead area, it can compound an already difficult low-on-gas situation.

The goal of any SCUBA configuration is to create a system that, when empty, is as near to neutral as possible and that, when completely full, is not excessively heavy. It stands to reason, then, that at the outset of a dive, one's cylinders will be much heavier because they will be full. How heavy they will be, though, depends on the type of cylinder and the gas mixture. For example, leaving aside the weight of the tanks, air in a set of double 80cf tanks would weigh more than 12 pounds, while the same volume of helium would weigh about three pounds.

Proper weighting involves balancing a number of factors; these include: increased surface buoyancy (particularly in a neoprene suit before compression), the weight of one's breathing supply (reduced as the dive continues), and the need to remain neutral at 10' (3m) assuming an empty set of cylinders. Typically, more than 80% of the weight a diver wears to sink a neoprene suit is needed only within the first atmosphere. After reaching this depth, compression of the material forces the diver to offset this weight with additional lift from the BC. Furthermore, this diver must also wear enough weight to counteract an empty set of tanks near the surface where the neoprene suit will again begin to exert additional lift. The additional weight necessary to accomplish these goals could easily leave a diver nearly 40 pounds negative at depth, making a buoyancy failure a potentially serious problem.

Diver Wearing 80cf Cylinders In Full Wet Suit

Weight of Tanks with Air In Double 80's	-6 pounds
Weight Worn to Offset Neoprene Suit	-25 pounds
Total Negative Weight	-31 pounds

As a worst-case scenario, imagine a failure occurring early in the dive that would cause the diver to have no control over buoyancy; e.g., what would occur if the air was not tuned on, the BC was not connected or the BC failed. Here the diver would be weighted down by both the weight required to offset surface buoyancy and the weight of the gas in the cylinders. In this situation, the diver should be able to remove enough weight (in the form of a weight belt or a canister light) to enable him/her to swim to the surface.

There are several ways to weight a diving rig; these include weight belts, canister lights, v-weights (placed beneath the back plate on doubles), and Keel™ weights (placed on the back of a single tank).[18]

Removable weight that allows divers to remove some of their weight (as opposed to all at one time) allows greater control over a buoyant ascent. This weighting may take the form of a removable canister used with a weight belt, or may utilize the Active Control Ballast system which allows divers to remove half of their ballast.[19] Depending on how much weight one needs, divers might choose to use a combination of fixed and removable weight, e.g., a combination of a v-weight and a canister light. Nonetheless, it is important not to overweight the diving rig with too much fixed weight, because it will prevent one from "ditching" the weight and swimming to the surface in the event of an emergency.

Far too many people assume that an easy solution to the weighting problem is to wear a lot of additional weight and then counteract that weight with oversized double wings. Not only will this "solution" leave a diver carrying far too much weight, it will also put him/her in the unenviable position of having to struggle with increased resistance caused by

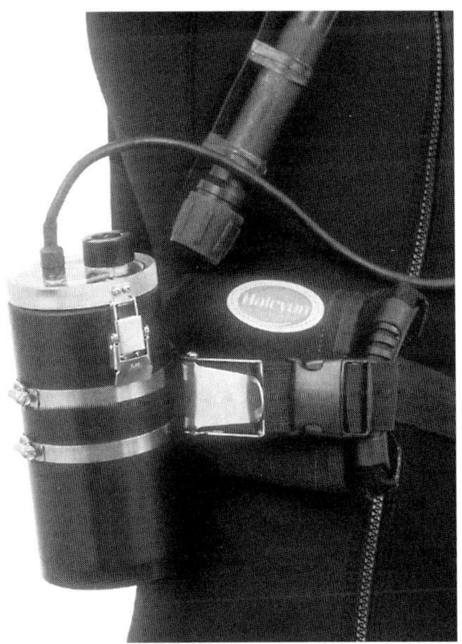

Halcyon Active Control Ballast system of ditchable weight.

[18] The Keel™ weight places weight on the back of the diver's tank to redistribute the diver's weight and/or counteract the positive buoyancy of a cylinder that would force a diver's face into the water if unconscious at the surface.

[19] ACB™ allows divers to maintain control over weighting while removing part or all of the detachable weight. Divers that find themselves over weighted but with ample air supply might choose to drop half of their ballast, providing for a more controlled ascent. Similar results are possible where divers might choose to drop a light canister.

the unnecessary drag of an oversized BC filled with too much air. As we mentioned earlier, trying to solve the weighting problem by resorting to a double BC system creates more problems than it solves because, while a diver is VERY unlikely to ever have a BC failure, the diver who opts for a double BC system will always be victimized by increased stress and task loading. Furthermore, should this system fail, the latter diver will be in substantially more trouble than the one who, from the outset, had configured their system to survive a loss of buoyancy. [20]

The ideal configuration for a diver is one that, while being as light as possible, allows him/her to remain neutral at 10' (3m) with a nearly empty set of tanks (to allow for decompression/safety stops). Quite often the only way to ensure this is to incorporate removable weights. Most divers carry this weight in the form of a belt that, in the event of an emergency, can be dropped; others carry this weight in the form of a canister light, which also can be dropped in the event of an emergency.

The bottom line here, however, is that divers should be certain that, without any air in their buoyancy compensators, they are capable of swimming against the weight of their configuration with full tanks and all weight in place. This would allow them to verify that they are able to manage their SCUBA configuration in the event of a buoyancy failure.

Choosing A Cylinder

Choosing the appropriate cylinder depends on several factors; e.g., body size, breathing rate, dive profile and diving environment. Selecting the wrong cylinder contributes to buoyancy control problems, and because of this, to environmental damage and diver risk. Failure to match the appropriate cylinders with the right exposure suit and buoyancy control system can also prove fatal. Most people find that Pressed Steel 104cf steel tanks are great for cave or cold water diving, where heavy thermal insulation and dry suits offset negative weighting. For longer dives or larger divers, 120's are also a popular choice.

For ocean diving in a wet suit, twin aluminum 80's are the cylinders of choice. Divers should never risk their life by being over weighted at the beginning of a dive. If one needs more gas, then they should take an aluminum stage. The buoyancy characteristics of aluminum, especially when filled with helium, are such that an added weight belt and/or canister light provides the necessary ballast that allows the rig to be only

[20]For more on the dangers associated with the double BC system, review the earlier discussion of BCs.

reasonably negative when full, neutral when empty, and capable of being swum if the weight is dropped. In cave diving, steel tanks are commonly used with a dry suit, because they must be negative enough to allow the diver to stay down in a low-on-gas emergency. There is nothing worse than being too light to stay off the ceiling while being low on gas and struggling. For this reason, prior to use, a rig must be balanced and weighted to accommodate a no-gas situation.

The diver must choose the type of tanks best suited to a particular diving environment.

©Achim Schlöffel, Croatia

Aggressive dives like those conducted in deep water or in overhead environments require ample reserve breathing supplies. Therefore, individuals often prefer larger volume, lower pressure, steel cylinders made by manufacturers like Pressed Steel and Faber; these generally have a working pressure of 2,640 psi.[21] The lower pressure tanks do not require high pressure fills to achieve a reasonable gas supply, but allow for higher volumes when necessary. This is especially useful for partial pressure Nitrox and Trimix fills. Divers using steel tanks should use additional buoyancy in the form of a dry suit to protect them from BC failures.

Cylinder Coating

When considering steel tanks, divers should be aware that some manufacturers "spray galvanize" their tanks. Spray galvanizing does not always

[21] Pressed Steel has recently re-rated these tanks for higher working pressures, making them an ideal combination that allows divers to choose lower pressures for ample gas supply or higher pressure for additional reserve.

provide a consistent coat, thereby making the cylinder more vulnerable to rust. Other manufacturers "hot dip galvanize" their cylinders, thereby creating a more even coat, and significantly reducing the risk of rusting. Pressed Steel tanks, such as distributed by PSI and Seagate, are the most popular "hot dip" tanks on the market; sprayed tanks include OMS and Faber. Aluminum tanks are typically painted or "brushed," and as such are much more resistant to the corrosive effects of many environments.

Dive Lights

Primary Lights

The kind of dive light one uses usually depends on the environment in which one dives and the particular diving activity in which one is engaged. However, the basic DIR configuration uses a single primary light canister attached to the diver's hip, and two reserve lights clipped to the diver's chest D-rings where they are held to the harness by two elastic bands. The size and weight of the canister light usually depends on the particular diver's needs. Lights are optional for shallow open water diving; however, most experienced divers prefer the versatility offered by the above configuration, even for open water diving. Divers should use primary lights with a beam that can be focused. This focused beam gives divers a better visual reference and provides the diver with an excellent means of communicating with other team members. The primary light is very useful in open water diving as a signalling device, and is also very handy should a properly trained team encounter an overhead or need illumination in a darkened recess.

The primary light canister is worn on the right side of the waist belt, adjacent to the backplate, and is held securely there beneath the shoulder by either the waist belt buckle or by a second buckle that is slid up behind it. The light is part of a diver's weight and balance, and should

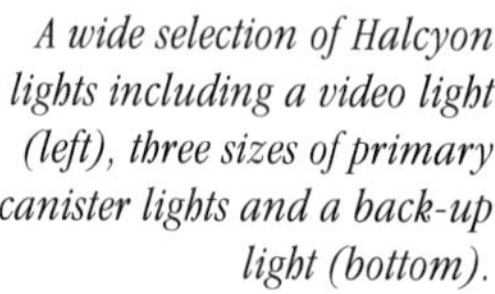

A wide selection of Halcyon lights including a video light (left), three sizes of primary canister lights and a back-up light (bottom).

be placed under the shoulder where it is protected and out of the flow, and can be conveniently operated or removed if necessary. This location not only keeps the light canister from interfering with a diver's kicking movement, but also places it in the same water column as the one broken by the diver's shoulder as s/he moves through the water. This insures that the light is streamlined and does not impede a diver's progress through the water. When the light is in use, the light head should be held in the left hand. When the light is not in use or when one's hands are needed to switch to a stage bottle or to a decompression bottle, the light head should be clipped off to the right chest D-ring.

An alternative to a waist-mounted light is to hang the canister from the bottom of one's tanks; this alternative should be altogether avoided. Butt-mounting places the canister below the tanks where, especially if the canister is flooded, it tends to drag a diver's legs down. This would effectively undermine the cardinal rule of diving, which maintains that a good diver must preserve a "feet up," horizontal trim to maximize efficiency, reduce the risk of disturbing sediments, and prevent damage to local environments. Lights attached below the tanks, alongside the harness, or in other locations disturb balance, waste valuable storage areas, diminish diver control and prevent easy removal of the light.

Proper position of the waist-mounted canister light.

Some people believe that divers with hip-mounted lights cannot efficiently wear multiple stage bottles. Nothing is further from the truth. A glance at the configuration of today's most active explorers will suffice to put these concerns to rest. Not only do they wear a hip-mounted light, they also carry two, three, four or more stage bottles with unparalleled efficiency. In such a configuration, a multiple stage dive is conducted with all stage bottles located on the left side of the body, opposite the light canister. This allows divers more flexibility, because one of their arms will always be unencumbered. In this fashion, divers find it easier to pilot a scooter and to work through smaller areas with stage bottles intact.

Reserve Lights

Reserve or back-up lights are key components of the DIR gear configuration. These lights must be reliable, streamlined and conveniently stowed. Following a primary light failure in an overhead environment, the diver must switch to the reserve light and initiate an exit. Ideally, the time spent on a reserve light should not be greater than half of a diver's bottom time; nonetheless, a reserve light should be able to provide more time in the event of a delayed exit. Reserve lights whose burn times equal a diver's total bottom time would be excellent choices.[22] While primary lights should contain rechargeable batteries, reserve lights should contain disposable batteries. This is because disposable batteries have a more reliable burn time, and provide consistent and predictable results. Reserve light batteries should be replaced after each significant use or after six months if not used at all. The old batteries should be fine for household use, but are no longer reliable for critical life-support.

Reserve lights should be stored on the harness below the arms, where they tuck neatly out of the way and are essentially snag-free. A diver with a primary light failure can easily turn on the reserve light before removing it. The benefits of this are clear; if the light has been turned on before it is unclipped and dropped it can be easily found. Also, another advantage of positioning the reserve light in this manner is that it can be activated and left clipped off while one is managing other equipment. In short, reserve lights configured in this manner are easier to remove, easier to activate, easier to replace and do not require additional attachments, like clamps and D-rings, on the tank. Mounting lights on the tank inhibits easy access, limits the ability to see if the

---

[22] Divers should also avoid lights that overdrive the bulb with excess voltage. Most manufactures utilize this technique in an attempt to make the lights appear brighter. This places undue stress on the bulb and may result in a failure. Reserve lights made by Extreme Exposure are made specifically to prevent this problem.

light has been knocked on and requires that the light be removed prior to turning it on. This should always be avoided.

Stage/Decompression Bottles

A stage bottle is a bottle used to extend bottom time, whereas a decompression bottle is a bottle used during the ascent portion of the dive to promote efficient decompression by reducing inert gases (e.g., N_2 and He) while elevating oxygen percentages. Stage and decompression bottles are almost exclusively used in technical diving, where longer bottom times and/or multiple gas mixes are the standard. These bottles usually rely on the same or similar equipment and are filled with appropriate gases for a given dive.

While ocean diving, stage and decompression bottles should be made of aluminum so as to not overweight the diver. Because conditions in the ocean are unpredictable, diving in the ocean should be limited to 90 minutes of total immersion and less should conditions warrant. For this reason, cylinders as small as 40cf are usually perfectly adequate for most ocean decompressions, with 80cf cylinders being the permissible upper limit.

In cave diving, where decompression bottles are left behind in the spring basin, steel bottles are appropriate. Cave divers usually prefer steel bottles because their lower working pressure provides them with a better volume of oxygen for the given pressure (i.e., a steel 95cf bottle contains 95cf of oxygen at 2,640psi, whereas at 2640psi a 80cf cylinder will only hold 72cf of oxygen). In cave diving, the decompression cylinders of choice are steel 72's or steel 95's for oxygen, and aluminum 80's

For ocean diving, aluminum stages are required to prevent overweighting;

for Nitrox mixes. For buoyancy reasons specified earlier, all stage bottles (those used for penetration diving) should be aluminum 80's or their international equivalent.

All stage and decompression bottles should be rigged with stainless steel bolt snaps; what size these will be is determined by whether or not one's diving requires gloves. Steel bolt snaps are attached by a piece of 1/4" line run under a hose clamp placed halfway down the tank. The upper bolt snap should be placed slightly above the break of the neck and sit snugly against the tank. The lower bolt snap should be affixed to the 1/4" line that will extend beyond the hose clamp. This tie point for the snap should be near the middle of the bottle (roughly 16 inches between clip attachments). To prevent drag, the bottle needs to be held close in the front and relatively loose in the back. If the bottom clip is placed too low or is affixed too tightly, then the bottom of the bottle will be pulled higher, and will form a wedge with the front of the bottle. Cylinders should float horizontally and sit parallel to a prone diver.

Uniform stage bottle marking simplifies equipment management both in and out of the water.

©Anthony Rue

There should NEVER be any metal-to-metal connections of any part of one's equipment. Stage bottle clips MUST be able to be cut free should the clip jam or the bottle become entangled.

All bottles should be permanently marked to reflect their maximum operating depth (MOD), using three-inch high letters placed horizontally in the orientation of the tank. Furthermore, tanks should be marked on both sides to allow both the diver and his/her buddy to take note of the depth, regardless of tank position. Markings other than MOD (e.g., Nitrox stickers) merely clutter a diver's bottle and fail to provide any useful information. For example, a Nitrox sticker tells one nothing about what percentage of oxygen the cylinder contains or how deep the tank is to be used.

A decompression or stage bottle regulator is fitted with a short pres-

Left: Stage bottle showing stainless steel bolt snaps attached with 1/4" line. There are no metal-to-metal connections anywhere of the cylinder. Note the length of "tail" attaching the lower snap. The MOD is permanently marked in three-inch high letters in a horizontal orientation on both sides of the cylinder.
Center: The SPG is mounted on a short (six inch) hose and bent back on itself, facing the diver. It is held in place by bungie cord.
Right: The regulator is mounted on an octopus-length (38") hose, which is tucked beneath an elastic band when not in use.

sure gauge bent back on itself to face the diver, and is held in place, at the first stage, by bungie cord. Its hose must be octopus length, or 38" (15cm). When not in use, regulators are always tucked away in an elastic band on the bottle, and the bottle turned off.

To facilitate streamlining and one-hand valve management, decom-

Diver carrying an O_2 bottle, viewed from the side and the front.

pression/stage bottles are generally worn on the left side. Wearing bottles on both sides forces a diver's arms into a bulky "muscle man" posture and greatly limits flexibility. In addition to limiting diver flexibility, stages on a diver's right side interfere with efficient DPV piloting.[23]

To deploy a bottle, divers should carefully adhere to the following procedure:

1. Divers should operate as a team, verifying proper mixture and depth.
2. Arrive at the desired switching depth, retrieve and attach the cylinder if required (i.e., in a cave dive where bottles are left behind).
3. Locate the properly marked cylinder and deploy its second stage (regulator is stored in a retaining band on the cylinder). Open the valve completely.
4. Each diver should double-check their buddy's cylinder depth and the second stage used.
5. Remove regulator from the mouth and replace with stage regulator.
6. Grab the second stage hose and retrace it back to the stage cylinder.
7. Double-check cylinder marking.
8. If beginning decompression, start decompression time.

Scooter Diving

Underwater propulsion vehicles can be remarkable assets to a variety of diving activities. By allowing divers to cover great distances while reducing effort and air consumption, scooters offer divers incredible tools to work with underwater. Technical divers often use scooters, but scooter diving can be a great deal of fun for any diver in any environment. The most versatile form of propulsion vehicle is the "tow behind" scooter and should be preferred to the ride-on, torpedo-style scooter. The latter presents special problems: 1) because the propeller is beneath the diver, it can "eat" gear, 2) both the scooter and the diver need to break the wa-

[23] **Advanced Technical Diver Note:** Two bottles can easily be worn on a diver's left side. Depending on the intended purpose of these bottles, divers carrying more than two bottles have several options. If these are to be carried a short distance (e.g., an oxygen bottle that will be dropped at the cave entrance), then they can be temporarily clipped to their top right D-ring. If properly weighted, the bottle will easily find its own horizontal position in the short trip to the entrance. Alternatively, divers can clip the clip at the neck to their hip. Bottles that are properly weighted will sit effectively in this position. Divers from the WKPP and GUE sometimes carry more than a dozen bottles by clipping them in sets to a tank-carrying loop, each connected by a single clip to the D-ring.

ter, and any added bottles or gear must in turn also break the water, 3) it must be maneuvered by "body English," which results in higher gas consumption, and 4) it makes towing a diver or additional gear (bottles and/or scooters) difficult. On the other hand, tow behinds entail none of these problems: 1) they break the water in front of the diver so that the diver and his gear are somewhat in the slipstream of the scooter, 2) the props are in front of the diver where he can be seen, 3) they are very maneuverable, and 4) they facilitate equipment.

When scooter diving, one must reconcile a scooter's speed and power with one's ability to return to safety without it, should it fail. In fact, not only can too much speed sabotage one's gas planning, it also cannot be accurately estimated when planning for a towing emergency. Furthermore, too much speed over distance causes thermal problems for the diver, navigation problems for cave diving, and breathing problems. Lastly, since power required for speed rises exponentially, and drag rises exponentially with speed, then there is an immediate point of diminishing returns where the battery capacity required to burn even a short time at high speeds becomes prohibitive.

Scooters need to be easy to work on and easy to clear of hydrogen gas from batteries. The best scooters these days have removable lids and o-rings, and can be repaired in the field. Since the re-uptake reaction of a gel cell or lead acid battery is, by definition, carried out in gas form, expect some hydrogen gas to be released from the batteries at charging and discharging. It is a good idea to vent the scooter batteries for an hour before sealing the scooter for use. It is also always a good idea not to seal the scooter for use until ready to dive, and to unseal it immediately following the dive.

Components of the scooter must be in proper working order. First,

Scooter diving in a cave. Note the towed back-up scooter.

©Steve Auer

one should test the batteries' longevity or "burn time." This is accomplished by what is called a "burn test," a test that establishes the burn time of the batteries, by using a set of resistors to simulate the current draw of the motor. If batteries get hot while charging or discharging, they should be immediately replaced. Second, the motor seal and the seals between the battery and motor compartments should be checked for integrity by a vacuum test.

A scooter's propeller assembly must incorporate a clutch assembly that will allow the blades to slip should the assembly become entangled. A slip clutch allows the scooter to still be used if the motor sticks on; when one needs to stop, the blades can be stopped and adjusted to zero pitch, and then reset to run. A scooter's blades must generally be pinned with a steel pin and replaced if the fittings wear out. A variable-pitch blade system allows one to fine-tune one's speed-to-load ratio without subjecting oneself to the risk and hassle of electronic speed or pulse control methods. Simpler in propulsion is always better, especially in aggressive diving environments. Metal blades have too much mass and exert so much pressure on the clutch spring that they generally cause the shear pin to be lost before the clutch will slip. If the clutch does not slip, the motor cannot spin freely in the event of propeller entanglement; this in turn may lead to a relay or other failure because the motor will try to spin the locked blades.

The best method of attaching a scooter is by a tow cord that runs from the scooter handles to the front D-ring on the diver's crotch strap. This configuration allows the diver to be pulled by the D-ring attachment and not by the arms. This allows his/her hands to remain relaxed, with only wrist action required to guide the scooter, a finger on the trigger. The best position for the scooter is where the propeller wash will not hit the diver at all. The best handle position is riding with the scooter out in front, the arm extended but relaxed, the hand lying on the handle.

The protocol for towing a diver with a disabled scooter is to first stow the disabled scooter. This is done by threading the disabled scooter's tow cord through its forward lifting handle (near the nose of the scooter) and using the excess loop with the attached bolt snap to clip off onto the diver's rear D-ring. Thus, the diver tows his own scooter while holding onto his buddy's D-ring, and being towed himself. The towed diver must resist the temptation to look where he is going; by keeping his head down s/he will generate less drag. This protocol is also used for towing one or more scooters.

©Sandra Edwards

Correct method of attaching the scooter tow cord.

Divers in overhead environments, e.g., a cave, might encounter areas that do not allow for continued use of a DPV. This dictates that scooters be left behind. Protocol for leaving scooters in the water includes first pinning the trigger, and then turning the blades back to no pitch. This will reduce the likelihood that a scooter will accidentally activate itself and ruin the visibility and/or damage the guideline. This also holds true when towing a scooter.

Gas "rules" for scooter diving in caves can be replaced with a review of objectives: 1) maintain sufficient gas reserves that would allow a diver to swim out of a cave in the event of a scooter failure; 2) carry a backup scooter (and a buddy) in order to get out in the event a scooter fails, 3) place safeties, or 4) and the best method, is to have twice the scooter burn time and twice the gas needed. Safety scooters should be placed at stage drops and should only be burned for about 33% of their capacity in one direction before they are switched. The reasoning here is that, in light of this, barring a catastrophe, divers will never be without a scooter; any scooter will then get them back to one of their last scooters. Even if one breaks, the scooter a diver will be riding will have a 33% reserve to get them to the next one; all of the scooters have power left.

Computer Diving

Divers have three primary methods by which to calculate dive and/or decompression time, namely, tables, wrist-mounted computers, and personal computer decompression programs. There is a great deal of debate surrounding the use of wrist-mounted decompression computers; divers wear these to calculate dive time limitations and decompression obliga-

A digital bottom timer, when used in conjunction with dive tables and/or a personal computer decompression program, is preferred over the use of a dive computer

©ScubaPro

tions during the dive. Some educators have discussed abandoning the learning of decompression tables, which is very similar to eliminating the teaching of basic math skills—like addition and subtraction—in favor of a calculator.

The most obvious problem with diving a computer is that, should the computer fail, a diver would be left without essential diving information. All divers should learn the proper use of decompression tables in order to learn the actual process of decompression diving. Divers that choose to use computers should do so after becoming well-versed in diving limits and then using the computer primarily as an educational tool. The following list includes concerns about decompression computers.

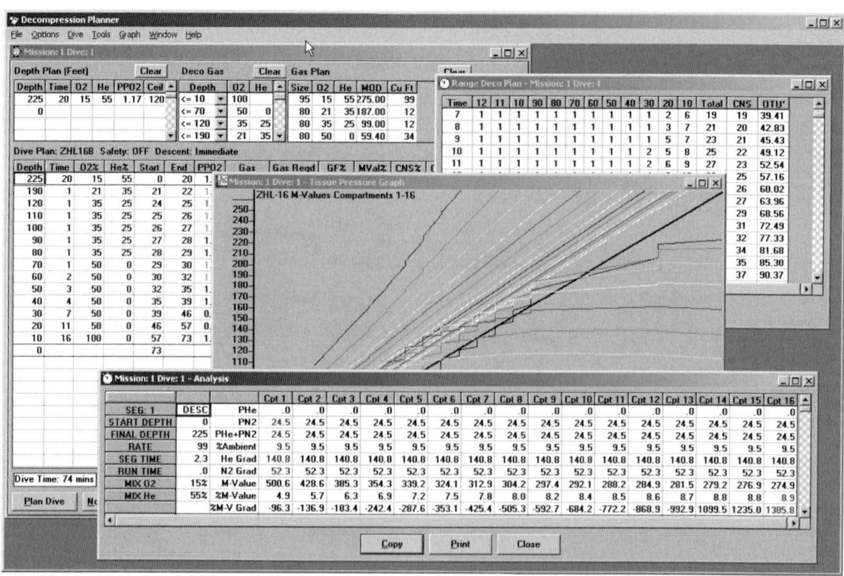

Global Underwater Explorer's DecoPlanner is at the forefront of decompression software.

A Baker's Dozen: Problems With Computer Diving

1. Dive computers tend to induce significant levels of diver dependence, and undermine the awareness essential to all diving, but particularly essential to divers just beginning decompression diving.
2. Dive computers prohibit proper planning; they discourage divers from "studying" the impact of various mixtures and decompression choices.
3. Dive computers are of little educational benefit because they promote neither questioning nor proper planning discussions.
4. Dive computers often use algorithms that heavily pad decompression time; this sometimes results in odd and ridiculous levels of conservatism.
5. Dive computers are expensive, and prevent divers with limited resources from purchasing truly useful equipment.
6. Dive computers significantly limit the likelihood that divers will track their residual nitrogen groups, leaving them less informed in the event of computer failure.
7. Dive computers do not allow for diving helium in any format but the bulkiest and most questionable. It is very likely that new helium-based decompression computers will be inordinately conservative and suffer from all the limitations of air and Nitrox dive computers.
8. Dive computers often generate longer decompressions than an astute, well-educated, experienced diver generates.
9. Dive computers often confuse matters by providing the diver with too much useless information, sometimes even obscuring depth and time in favor of blinking CNS and/or decompression limitations.
10. Some dive computers become very difficult to use if a decompression stop has been violated. Some computers will lock up completely, while others will just beep or generate erroneous and distracting information.
11. Dive computers do not allow the educated diver to properly modify his/her decompression profile to account for advances in knowledge, e.g., the use of deeper stops in a decompression profile.
12. Dive computers do not offer divers much flexibility to generate profiles with varying conservatism. For example, the right mix would allow 100 minutes at 60 ft rather than 60 minutes at 60 ft, but a diver might prefer to do one or the other or a hybrid of the two. Computers confuse this issue by not providing divers with the proper information.
13. Dive computer users often ignore table proficiency and therefore do not learn to read tables properly. When faced with a situation where they can't dive a computer (e.g., failure or loss) these divers are seriously handicapped.

The Body

The body is the central component to any effective diving locker, and no discussion of equipment would be complete without giving it a mention. Many debates have revolved around the necessity of fitness in diving, and no doubt these debates will continue for years to come. It seems that the most reasonable course is to evaluate the type of diving to be done and adjust the fitness level accordingly. The average diver should be seeking good cardiovascular fitness with aerobic activity AT LEAST three days a week for a minimum of 30 minutes. However, good fitness can serve a diver in life as well as diving, and a thorough fitness routine will leave one more prepared for the rigors of diving. A person winded by climbing a flight of stairs can certainly dive, but their ability to manage stressful, gas critical situations is limited by their ability to physically respond to elevated exertion. This may seem inconsequential on a leisurely dive, but in an emergency it can make all the difference.

©David Rhea, Ginnie Springs, Florida

©Steve Auer

©Barry Miller/GUE, Kea, Greece

Technical diving opens up a new world of underwater exploration. With the addtion of advanced skills, opportunities to participate in activities like deep wreck and cave exploration can be found around the world.

Top:Technical diving skills include managing double cylinder configurations, dry suit diving, and decompression gas management.

Middle: GUE exploration divers Todd Kincaid and Tyler Moon survey the props of the HMS Britannic.

Bottom: Woodville Karst Plain Project divers in the cave system at Indian Springs, Florida.

©Steve Auer

CHAPTER 7

ARE YOU READY FOR TECHNICAL DIVING?

In earlier chapters, we discussed the importance of natural ability and of sound basic diving skills to all forms of diving. Nonetheless, to some degree, the type of diving one does determines the level of excellence a diver must develop in each of these basic skills. In other words, an unforgiving environment, such as a cave or a wreck, demands a degree of excellence in buoyancy control that is not demanded by a forgiving environment, like a Bonaire reef dive. This means that, though the basic skills necessary for technical diving are identical to those necessary for recreational diving, the degree of precision and ability required in each of these areas rises dramatically the more demanding the environment becomes.

GUE Instructor Ted Cole using the Halcyon semi-closed rebreather.

©Ron De Amorim

Most divers, educators, and organizations underestimate the degree of skill required to dive competently in any given environment, whether that be recreational or technical. In any given year, roughly 60% of all fatalities involve divers with a total of twenty dives or less (B&E pp. 240). This statistic demonstrates that, historically, the risk of fatality rises or drops with personal experience and competence. This is also true of both DCI and gas embolism incidents where more than half of the victims were inexperienced (B&E pp. 240). This link between risk and inexperience suggests that, to reverse this trend, the

Elliott, D. H. and Bennett, P. B. "Underwater Accidents." The Physiology and Medicine of Diving. 4th Ed., pp. 238-252. Ed. P. Bennett & D. Elliott. London: W. B. Saunders Co. Ltd. 1993 diving community must commit itself to a more robust training curriculum, one that not only cultivates skill development, but also underscores the need for diving experience.

With respect to technical diving (such as deep, overhead or mixed gas), it is unlikely that many recreational divers have the requisite knowledge, skill, attitude and judgment to pursue it safely. Most divers are not willing to invest the necessary time and energy to develop the skills that will enable them to be successful in aggressive diving environments. Though there are few commonly recognized prerequisites for being able to meet the demands of technical diving, successful technical divers, and students who successfully complete rigorous training programs, typically share the following traits:

- Experience
- Ability
- Fitness

How Much Experience Should I Have Before Taking a Technical Diving Course?

Divers with more experience are in a better position to manage the rigorous demands of certain environments. Divers who lack experience, who are still weak in their basic skills, are often overly taxed by the burdens of aggressive environments. A significant number of individuals who are successful in technical diver training are dive masters, instructors, or individuals with comparable leadership-level training. This does not mean, however, that these students of technical diving were successful because they were certified dive masters or instructors; what it does mean is that because they were willing to invest the requisite time, money and energy to develop the experience and skill set that would allow them to be dive masters and instructors, they were more likely to succeed in a technical diving course. In other words, what is necessary for success in a technical diving course is experience and sound basic diving skills, not a particular certification.

Career Total

Entry-level technical divers should be frequent divers. They should be logging at least 75 SCUBA dives each year and have approximately 100 dives total. More advanced forms of technical training require more experience. This means that for each level of technical training, i.e., entry, intermediate, and advanced, one should have a minimum number of dives, i.e., 100, 200 and 300, respectively. Many people need more experience than is indicated by these estimates.

Recent Experience

Before considering a course in technical diver training, divers should be diving actively and without interruption. Active diving, followed by a long sabbatical, will leave a diver with rusty skills and unable to manage the rigors of technical diver training. Successful students typically log at least 20 dives within six months of their class.

What buoyancy skills should I master before taking a technical diving course?

An extended-range cave dive may require the use of several stage and decompression bottles as well as multiple DPVs.

©Ron De Amorim, Wakulla Springs, Florida

Students who do well in technical diver training typically practice and master the buoyancy skills outlined on this page. They do so in confined or open water, 30 days before the start of their course.

Weighting

Prospective students should be able to weight themselves so that, at the end of a dive, with 500 psi in their tanks, and little or no air in their BCs, they can hover motionless at a safety-stop depth. Divers using steel cylinders may need some air in their BCs, but should be sure that they are not unnecessarily weighted.

Body Position

Students should be able to position themselves, by shifting tank and weight system height, into a perfectly horizontal hover. Students can test this by seeing if they can view everything that is going on behind them simply by tucking their chins to their chests.

HELICOPTER TURN
While in the above position, students should be able to complete a 360-degree turn, simply by sculling with their ankles and fins. The rest of the body, especially the hands, should remain motionless throughout the turn.

HOW IMPORTANT IS PHYSICAL FITNESS TO THE TECHNICAL DIVER?

Technical diving is a physically demanding activity. In an emergency, personal fitness can literally make the difference between life and death; it is also a key factor in reducing the risk of decompression illness. Successful technical divers are typically committed to the following state of health and fitness.

DIET/BODY MASS
During a typical day, technical divers have a fairly good feel for their total caloric intake, as well as for the number of proteins, carbohydrates and fats they consume. Fatty foods, what one would typically find at a fast-food restaurant, do not factor into their diet. Technical divers have little difficulty maintaining a body weight that is in proportion to their height, sex and build. Their percentage of body fat, relative to total body mass, is well below that of the typical recreational diver.

EXERCISE
A technical diver's minimum aerobic workout consists of at least 20 minutes a day, three days a week; 30 minutes every day is better. In general, exercise is something divers make time for, not something they do when they have time.

LIFESTYLE
Smoke tobacco? Forget training at advanced technical levels. Substance dependency? Don't even think about it. Like to stay up late and party? Not if you want to dive the next day.

GENERAL HEALTH
Students should either be able to answer every question on the RSTC Medical History/Exam Form with an unqualified "No," or have a signed physician's approval for diving. This should be based on a physical exam that was given within the last twelve months, and meets RSTC/UHMS guidelines.

How do you stack up against the above criteria? If you can honestly say, "Yes, that's me," you may be ready for the rigors of technical training. If you meet some of these criteria, but not all of them, you should reconsider technical diving, or consult a professional to establish how to properly prepare for technical training. Finally, if you find yourself coming up short in more than just one or two of these areas, accept the fact that the rigors of a hostile diving environment may not be for you. Though this is something most people do not want to hear, it is simply the truth. Technical diving does not have to be more dangerous than any other forms of diving; whatever risks exist are usually the result of an individual's choices. These choices start well before divers enter the water; to choose to be in the water when one is ill equipped to do so is to expose oneself to a foolish and unnecessary level of risk.

©Steve Auer, Wakulla Springs, Florida

This underwater videographer is diving in an overhead environment while using a DPV and carrying a stage bottle, greatly increasing the complexity of his dive.114

Top left: GUE oceanic research team descending to 250 feet along the Bahama Bank as part of a deep reef survey effort; Top right: The Duke Center for Hyperbaric Medicine's main recompression chamber; Lower left: Liquid Oxygen storage used to drive the hyperbaric chamber at the Duke facility; Lower right: Decompression, stage and safety bottles are organized according to the depth they will be utilized prior to placement on the dive boat. On the boat, bottles will be organized by diver and dive team to maximize efficiency in getting the divers in the water.

Photos ©GUE

Chapter 8

Alternate Breathing Mixtures

Why Add Oxygen To Air?

The idea behind Nitrox is not so much to add oxygen, but to reduce nitrogen. It is nitrogen that really limits our diving, that accumulates in our tissues and reduces the time we can stay at depth without subjecting ourselves to mandatory decompression. Nitrox is an oxygen-enriched mixture that reduces the percentage of nitrogen in our breathing mixtures by increasing the percentage of oxygen found in that mixture; in contrast to air, which is (roughly) 21% oxygen and 79% nitrogen, 32% Nitrox contains (roughly) 32% oxygen and 68% nitrogen. With less nitrogen in the breathing mix the diver can enjoy longer bottom times with less risk of DCI.

What Is Nitrox?

Information about Nitrox can be broken down into the following:

1. Technically, Nitrox is any mixture of nitrogen and oxygen, but is more commonly considered to be an oxygen-enriched mixture.
2. Oxygen-enriched air has been actively used for more than 30 years, and has been theoretically known for more than 200 years.
3. Manipulating oxygen levels was essential to certain military operations, and, as early as WWII, became routine in commercial, scientific, and medical arenas.
4. In 1979, The National. Oceanic and Atmospheric Association (NOAA) released the first publicly available set of Nitrox tables, fuelling a debate over the use of Nitrox in the recreational communities.
5. Nitrox gained significant recreational popularity in the early 1990s.

Advantages of Breathing Nitrox

1. Bottom times and decompression obligations are tied to metabolically inert gas accumulation (such as nitrogen). Since Nitrox reduces the percentage of metabolically inert gas in a diver's breathing mixture, it can significantly influence bottom time.
2. Less nitrogen in the diver's breathing mix allows for longer bottom times and for safer dives. For example, the NDL for a 60-foot dive on Nitrox is 100 minutes in contrast to an air dive to the same depth

whose NDL is only 60 minutes.

3. Custom Nitrox mixtures allow divers to maximize their bottom times while reducing DCI risk.
4. With Nitrox, divers can choose longer dives and/or shorter decompression obligations with reduced decompression stress.

FIGURE 2: NO-DECOMPRESSION LIMITS WITH AIR AND NITROX

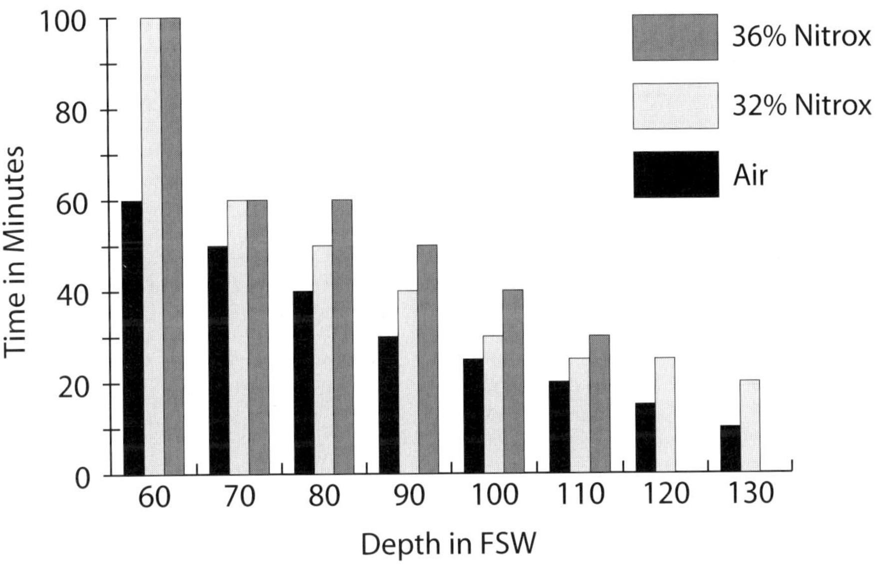

COMPLICATIONS OF USING NITROX

Our understanding of Nitrox is based on both scientific research and empirical evidence. Of course, the use of Nitrox is not without risk; like air diving, it has certain risks and limitations.

1. Nitrox does not eliminate the risk of DCS. Divers who take full advantage of its longer bottom times are not likely to greatly reduce their risk of DCS.
2. When divers do not respect the time and depth limitations of Nitrox, CNS oxygen toxicity can result in underwater seizure and drowning.
3. *Very* aggressive diving profiles may overextend the margin of safety with Nitrox.
4. *Very* extensive (very long and/or frequent) enriched air exposures can initiate lung damage, leading to pulmonary toxicity; *this is unlikely in recreational use.*

5. Compared to air, Nitrox has the same, if not (theoretically) greater, narcotic potential.
6. The greatest single hazard facing a Nitrox user is *oxygen toxicity* or *Central Nervous System Oxygen Toxicity* (CNS toxicity). Though oxygen is required to sustain life, too much of it can cause damage and even death; extensive exposures to oxygen-enriched mixtures can damage the pulmonary system. Nevertheless, the risk of this to the well-informed and responsible technical diver is negligible.

Nitrox Summary

Above 100 ft (30m) Nitrox has all but eliminated the need for air diving. That, combined with the introduction of helium for dives beyond 100 ft, means that in the near future—as diver appreciation of the advantages of proper mixtures continues to grow—air diving will be relegated to a historical curiosity. Indeed, even today, many experienced divers have trouble remembering the last time they used air as a diving mixture, having for a long time taken advantage of the safety and flexibility offered by Nitrox and helium mixtures.

Bottles containing decompression mixes including Nitrox and Trimix are grouped on the beach at Wakulla prior to being placed by WKPP support divers at designated decompression stops in the cave.

©Ron De Amorim, Ft. Lauderdale

Helium-Based Diving Gases

Helium is an inert gas that, for centuries, has been used by commercial and military deep-sea divers to allow them to work at depths where air would be debilitating. In the last ten years helium has become increasingly more popular among technical deep divers, and has a growing following among sport divers who wish to safely explore beyond 100 feet (30m). These divers are finding that helium allows them to enjoy safer, more pleasurable diving, as well as more efficient decompressions, reduced gas density and the elimination of dangerous narcosis.

Helium-based diving falls into three primary categories:

1. **Triox:** a helium-based gas with 21% or greater oxygen content
2. **Trimix:** any combination of oxygen, helium and nitrogen
3. **Heliox:** any combination of oxygen and helium

Breathing a helium-based gas with 21% oxygen content eliminates the risk that divers near the surface will experience hypoxia (not enough oxygen). Furthermore, *Triox* allows divers the benefit of helium-based gases without the need for travel gases or other decompression bottles. In short, a Triox gas can be dived very much like air but without any narcotic impairment. However, as divers approach 150 feet (45m) they must reduce the oxygen content below 21% or risk oxygen toxicity. In contrast, *Trimix* mixtures commonly have a reduced oxygen component so that they can be dived deep without the risk of oxygen toxicity. These commonly have oxygen contents from 10% to18% and helium contents from about 25% to 80%. However, a mixture with oxygen content lower than roughly 16% cannot be used near the surface without risking unconsciousness from hypoxia. Lastly, *Heliox* mixtures allow divers to eliminate all nitrogen and its associated risks (e.g., narcosis). Historically, Heliox has been used very deep, where even small amounts of nitrogen can cause narcosis. Due to their high helium content, Heliox mixtures are less common outside commercial applications; however, a growing number of technical divers are appreciating the benefit of high helium content in their breathing mixtures.

A gas mixing station used for mixing Nitrox and Trimix. The mixing station may be as simple or elaborate as the diver cares to make it.

©Anthony Rue

Lastly, the use of deep, helium-rich, mixtures—where oxygen is roughly less than 16%—can require additional gases for descent and decompression. In contrast to the "bottom mix," gas which is used at the maximum depth, these additional gases are called "travel mixes." Given their elevated oxygen content (appropriate to the required depth), these mixes not only allow divers safe conduct to depths where using their bottom mix is risk-free, but also function as one of a their decompression mixes (usually the deepest available mix that contains sufficient oxygen content).

Gas Narcosis

Narcosis is everyone's enemy, and its effects range from a subtle decrease in judgment to total incapacitation. Narcosis can be produced by a very wide variety of agents, from simple gases like xenon and nitrogen, to complex hydrocarbons used to produce general anaesthesia. Although the narcotic effect of gases has been studied for over 100 years, a full understanding of how they produce narcosis (and anaesthesia) is missing. In the case of nitrogen, much of what is known about its narcotic effect comes from the study of anaesthetic gases. Around 1900, Meyer and Overton independently observed that the potencies of general anaesthetic gases were tied to their solubility in a simple organic solvent, olive oil. These observations have become known as the Meyer-Overton rule; this predicts that *the anaesthetic potency of a gas is inversely related to its*

Table 5.1 Bunsen Solubility Coefficients for Common Gases

Gas	Bunsen Solubility Coefficient in Olive Oil, 22 C; ATA $^{-1}$
Helium	0.015
Hydrogen	0.042
Nitrogen	0.052
Oxygen	0.110
Argon	0.150
Krypton	0.440
Carbon Dioxide	1.340
Nitrous Oxide	1.560
Xenon	1.900

lipid solubility. In other words, more lipid-soluble gases produce narcotic effects at lower concentrations than less soluble gases. Table 5.1 lists Bunsen's solubility coefficients for common gases.

Thus, based on lipid solubility, helium should be the least narcotic and xenon the most narcotic gas; this is because in animals (including humans), the anaesthetic potency of these gases closely parallels their lipid solubility. Because of this, highly soluble gases, like nitrous oxide and xenon, can be used as anaesthetics at normobaric pressure.

Many divers believe that, through repetitive exposure, they can "adapt" to the effects of narcosis. However, an evaluation of divers breathing air at 54.6 meters (roughly 180 feet) once a day for five days, determined that there was no adaptation made; their reaction times remained constant, as did their procedural errors. However, over the same five days, there was a reduced perception of narcosis; this means that, although the divers *believed* themselves to be less impaired, there was no objective evidence to support this belief.

Conclusion

For more than 100 years, divers have been using mixtures other than air. In the last ten years, however, oxygen- and helium-enriched diving have started to become popular in the recreational and technical diving communities. This is because air is not an optimal breathing mix, plagued as it is with problems like narcosis, increased decompression and inefficient gas elimination. Today, for diving in the 30 to 100 foot (10-30m) range, an enriched oxygen mixture is the logical choice, while for diving deeper than 100 ft (30 m) a helium based mixture is optimal.

Despite its obvious inefficiencies, air is still popular with some divers because it is easier to find (there is a better infrastructure supporting air diving), and because of the force of habituation. Nonetheless, the future is surely one in which air diving will be looked at solely as a historical curiosity, not as a realistic alternative to sensible gas mixtures.

Lower left photo ©Steve Auer; all others ©GUE

DIR skills are equally important to the wreck diver, open water diver, and cave diver. Top: GUE instructor Richard Lundgren films the deck of the Britannic; Middle (left and right): drift diving along Bimini's coral reefs; Lower left: DIR cave team working on buddy skills.

CHAPTER 9

DIVING ENVIRONMENTS

The basic skills and techniques previously discussed in this text provide divers with a sound foundation for managing different diving environments. However, specialized environments demand specialized skills, and ever-greater refinement of those skills. Beyond sound basic skills, nearly every environment requires its own specific array of techniques, procedures, and equipment to safely deal with its demands. For example, exceptional open water divers, though they may possess superb basic skills, most likely will lack the specialized skills enabling them to manage safely and effectively in a cave environment; they will likely have problems navigating, communicating, and even positioning themselves efficiently in a cave. This type of problem is not unique to the open water diver; excellent cave divers may be as equally unprepared to go ice diving as open water divers are to go cave diving, or as ice divers are to go wreck diving. The point is that once a diver goes outside the scope of his/her training and experience, s/he will be less able to respond to the demands made by his/her new environment.

Environment-specific training provides individuals with the necessary skills and the required knowledge to safely engage a new environment and to begin learning. Quite often, the rules governing the safe exploration of a new environment are reasonably intuitive, such as the need to use a guideline in an overhead. Yet, divers without training consistently break these rules because they lack the requisite knowledge demanded by this new environment. These errors frequently result in fatalities, and ironically "surprise" other divers who perceived the victims as "experienced." In truth, divers, regardless of diving time, are only experienced in the specific environment to which they have become accustomed.

The competent diver, one who is knowledgeable and experienced in one environment, will oftentimes find learning to dive competently and safely in another environment much easier than someone who is not competent in any. Nonetheless, training is nearly always synonymous with safer diving. The following discussion outlines some general aspects of different diving environments,and is designed as an overview of these areas so that interested divers can better prepare for training in them.

Cave Diving

Cave diving is a very specialized form of technical diving. Like many types of specialty diving, the procedures for safe cave diving are relatively simple, but not necessarily intuitive. As such, all divers, regardless of proficiency, must engage in cave diver training to safely access the interior of a cave. Cave diver training is usually composed of several different courses, each building upon the training of the previous course.[1] Caves can vary from large open areas flooded by daylight (usually called caverns), to very extensive passages that can extend miles from the surface.[2] Some cave diving involves partially dry areas (called sumps), while other cave diving involves lava tubes. Caves are remarkable places filled with wonder and beauty; however, exploring them is not for everyone. Talented divers with sound basic diving skills should consider introductory training after reading more about what is required.

Divers seeking cave training should progress steadily through the training and ignore any encouragement to rapidly progress to the upper levels of cave certification. With respect to skill building, awareness, and teamwork, cave training is widely recognized as the best type of education that divers can receive. However, like most valuable skills, cave diving proficiency takes time and effort. Individuals that are interested in cave diving should focus on the process, not on the certification. Despite its likeness to many cave diving resources, in no way is this manual intended to be a cave diving resource. Divers who are interested in cave diving should visit www.gue.com, and on the basis of information there, consider whether they are suited for cave training.[3]

Cold Water

Some divers do not consider cold water diving an unusual form of diving; however, merely diving in cold water produces additional stresses and difficulties. Divers that are properly outfitted, in good thermal pro-

[1] GUE cave training comprises three courses from introductory to cave explorer level, and is the industry's most complete resource for cave diver education. Divers are encouraged to review the type of courses recommended for safe and effective training at www.gue.com.

[2] The world cave diving penetration record is currently nearly four miles in length, and is held by GUE president Jarrod Jablonski and WKPP Project Director George Irvine.

[3] Cf., GUE's Cave Diving Manual.

Cave diving demands the highest levels of skill and training– but the rewards are among diving's richest.

©Steve Auer, Tulum, Mexico

tection, are able to efficiently dive in areas that are near freezing. With the exception of good thermal protection, the equipment used in cold water diving is nearly identical to that of other properly configured DIR technical divers. Diving in cold water is undoubtedly more difficult and more dangerous than similar dives in warm water. Yet, with a good set of basic skills, most divers will be able to adapt well to this hostile environment.

Cold water diving presents its own array of problems, i.e., reduced decompression efficiency, increased danger associated with thermal failures (such as dry suits), and reduced manual dexterity from the numbing cold (particularly as the dive progresses). To some extent, regardless of whether they are consciously aware of it, all cold water divers experience some degree of stress associated with immersion. Diving in cold water also greatly increases the risks associated with being separated from the diving vessel, as divers who are separated can quickly develop critical hypothermia. Electric suits may allow divers more comfort in very cold water; however, given the possibility of failure, relying on these can be very problematic.

Other equipment failures include the freezing of regulators, dry suit or BC inflators. In very cold environments, where temperatures can plunge well below freezing (another reason to ensure all clips can be cut free, i.e., no metal-to-metal connections), clips and zippers may freeze on the surface. Simply spitting in one's mask can create freezing problems, as can trying to breathe a regulator on the surface. Breathing regulators at the surface can introduce humidity, which can promote freezing.

Ice Diving

Ice diving is obviously a subset of cold water diving, but in addition to good cold water skills, ice diving requires sound overhead diving skills. Cave diving training is often not required here, but it could be very beneficial to the ice diver, particularly if the diving goes beyond recreational exposures. If considering ice diving, individuals should seek training with a knowledgeable and experienced instructor, and seek to amass experience by diving with local ice divers. Several ice diving groups have carelessly approached ice diving and, in a number of different ways, lost their lives. When ice diving, individuals should be sure that the ice sheet is stable and thick enough to support the diving crew, and that all divers are tethered to the surface with support divers in position, prepared to assist.

Wreck Diving

Wreck diving lacks standardized training, and is taken up in a variety of different ways by different divers. Some recreational divers, for the most part, will only circle the exterior of a wreck, and will not penetrate the superstructure; others will penetrate deep into the interior using a set of techniques that they have borrowed (or not) from other specialized forms of diving. Though there are some instructors who offer wreck diving training, and some organizations that have classes on wreck diving, these are largely orientation courses, without overhead or advanced training principles.

Wreck penetration itself can vary; it can range from a cursory examination of areas that are easily accessible and close to the open water, to deep penetrations into the interior of the superstructure. Though there is no standardized training for this, most avid wreck divers pursue and

DIR techniques are just as at home in the icy waters of the Baltic Sea as the warm waters of the Caribbean.

©Ingemar Lundgren

recommend cave training as a means of developing a skill set that they will adapt to wreck penetration.[4] Cave training is very effective in preparing one for any overhead; nonetheless, divers should recognize that wrecks entail dangers that are absent from cave diving.

In many ways, wreck diving is inherently more dangerous than cave diving. Wreck dives are more susceptible to weather changes and to resulting water conditions. Furthermore, complications may prevent a wreck diver from returning to the dive boat and may lead to him/her being lost at sea or succumbing to frigid waters. On the other hand, the wrecks themselves are in a state of perpetual decomposition, and rife with decaying structures, entanglements, sharp edges, and marine life. Furthermore, wrecks often have multiple entrances and can confuse divers by allowing light to stream in from portholes and other false exits.

Diving From a Boat

Boat diving procedures can vary noticeably from one region to another. This is because some areas are consistently cursed with rough seas and heavy current, while others are blessed with continually flat seas and no current. Typically, conditions lie somewhere in between. The most important consideration in boat diving is to properly identify the risks and strive to eliminate or reduce them. For example, though all divers should strive not to be lost by the dive boat, divers diving deep in high current and cold water should be especially vigilant not to lose the support vessel, since being lost at sea in cold water could be potentially life threatening. Nonetheless, regardless of the situation, steps must always

GUE's surface support team assists divers before another pass on the Britannic.

©GUE, Kea, Greece

[4] GUE wreck diver training involves a combination of cave diving techniques and technical diver training.

be taken to ensure that both the team and the boat will be reunited at the end of the dive, and that emergencies will not leave the diving team stranded.

Anchor Diving

When conditions are good (moderate to low seas and light current), boats may choose to anchor in a particular spot while divers explore the surrounding area. The standard here is that divers usually head into the current at the beginning of the dive, and return to the boat with the current at the end of the dive. At a prearranged point (usually time and/or air supply will set this limit) the dive is "called," and the divers return to the boat. Obviously, anchor diving requires that the divers are able to swim against whatever current is present, and that the seas are sufficiently low so as not to produce unsafe boat conditions. High seas will abuse an anchored boat, and will not allow it to remain tethered in very rough conditions. Anchor diving must be done with a fixed diving location so that the dive team can stay near the boat.

Drift Diving with a Surface Marker

If sea conditions include strong currents and/or moderate to rough seas, dive operators will often (if conditions are safe) have the dive team drift with the current using a float ball or other obvious surface marker as a means of monitoring their progress. Divers drifting in the open ocean must have a surface marker to allow the boat to remain with them. Sur-

©Rebecca Fry

Divers drifting in the open ocean must carry adequate emergency flotation/signaling devices.

face currents can easily differ from currents at depth, making it impossible for a boat to know where the team is located without a surface marker. The dive boat will then float near the ball to provide support for the divers, and, in the event of traffic, notify vessels in the area that divers are below.

Heavy surface currents can pull a diver's float ball; when this occurs, a thin line to a surface dive flag will greatly reduce management difficulties. Drift diving with a surface marker is also difficult with multiple teams and/or bad weather (such as high seas or fog) since the boat may have trouble locating or maintaining contact with the dive team. Such conditions require multiple boats or a single team. Whenever there is doubt surrounding whether a boat can track a team, a new plan should be devised or the dive terminated.

Drifting into a Fixed Point

Occasionally, experienced technical divers will dive a location by drifting into a fixed point (like a wreck), explore the location, and terminate the dive at a fixed time/gas supply. The team can then shoot a lift bag or other surface marker to notify the boat of their changing position. In this situation, the boat would stay above the coordinates of the dive site until it sees the team's surface marker, and then drift with the team. This system is most commonly used when conditions like a strong current make it impractical to "hook" the location with a surface marker or up-line.

If the team is unsuccessful in locating their objective, they should terminate the dive and deploy a marker so that the boat can monitor their progress. Without a fixed dive site or surface marker, it can be very difficult for a boat to maintain contact with a dive team. Separation from the diving boat can be extremely dangerous, as teams in ocean currents may drift for miles; this can result in divers becoming lost at sea without the emergency support offered by a dive boat. Unfortunately, it is not uncommon for subsurface currents to vary from surface ones, which greatly increases the risk of diver separation. This means that drifting into a fixed point can involve the same difficulties as those discussed above (with diving with multiple teams), and must be managed accordingly.

Getting Back to the Boat

Divers have a variety of ways of exploring a dive site; however, all boat diving requires that divers are able to return to their diving vessel. In some situations, it is imperative to locate the dive boat; in others (such as near shore), it is less so. Nonetheless, divers should never get careless about locating the dive boat as it can be very difficult to find lost divers at sea, particularly in poor weather or low light conditions. In heavy currents or cold waters it becomes even more essential for divers to remain close to the diving vessel or to its chase boat.

Anchor diving is only done in limited or no current, making significant separation from the dive boat extremely unlikely. Likewise, drift divers must always have a surface marker, making it relatively simple for boat operators to maintain contact with them. Problems returning to the diving boat are most likely the result of diving a fixed point (a wreck) in heavy currents, or of drift diving where bad weather sets upon the dive team.

Divers that drift into a location, or that follow the anchor line to the wreck, must find their way back to the diving boat in one of several ways. If the dive boat is tied into the wreck, the team can make its way back up the fixed line (also called the up-line). If the dive boat is not attached to the wreck, then the dive team will commonly drift from the wreck and deploy a surface marker to allow the boat to stay with them. A similar situation often occurs with dive teams that are unable to return to the up-line due to high currents, misdirection, or emergencies.

Unable to Return to the Up-line

In some areas, divers prefer to tie into the wreck and use the anchor line to descend and ascend. However, if a team cannot reach the up-line because of an error or an emergency, it must either drift from the wreck and deploy a surface marker or attempt to fix a deployed marker to the wreck and ascend along this line. In moderate current, divers will not drift far from the diving spot; distant separation will then be unlikely. However, in high currents, divers drifting from the wreck could become substantially separated from the surface vessel. Nonetheless, attempting to ascend along a line fixed to the wreck in heavy current leaves the team exposed. It is generally preferable in these situations to drift from the wreck, deploy a surface marker, and allow the surface and/or chase boats to track the dive team.

Deploying a surface marker and drifting can be problematic should divers be in an area where very poor surface visibility (such as high waves and/or heavy fog) makes it hard to locate them. This situation may be compounded by dives where multiple teams are on a wreck and there are insufficient support vessels for one boat to follow each team. In such a scenario, divers may prefer to fix a line to the wreck and ascend along it, staying near the surface boat and limiting the risk of separation.

Surface Support

Lastly, it is important to note that adequate surface support is important to ensuring diver safety. Without adequate support, surface floats and/or deployed lift bags are difficult for a captain to spot and follow. The degree of support necessary depends on the particular conditions of the dive. For example, anchor diving in warm, shallow water with no current requires limited support. However, decompression dives in cold water with high currents require more robust support. Support divers can dive down an up-line and provide assistance (i.e., additional gas supply), and assist the captain in maintaining a fix on surface markers. Support is especially valuable when divers engage in decompression diving, as the potential for problems increases with the addition of more diving variables.

Where possible, it is beneficial for surface support personnel to have medical training, as they may provide life saving assistance during the initial phase of an emergency. Further, surface crews must possess some form of communication to arrange for emergency assistance. What type of communication will be needed, as well as how much surface support will be needed, will always depend on the environment and on the nature of the dive. For example, boat diving may use either a combination of maritime communication or cellular phones to establish good emergency communication, while land-based diving, such as those carried out in a lake or cave, might use a cellular phone or CB radio to do so.

WKPP Surface Manager Dawn Kernagis coordinates dive plans with Chris Werner before an exploration dive at Wakulla Springs.

©Anthony Rue

Decompression dives that are done in areas with high currents require a chase boat and good support diving personnel to guarantee safety and efficiency. Chase boats allow the primary dive vessel to remain fixed to the diving spot, while chase boats can split away and drift with drifting divers who were forced to abandon the up-line. Ideally, each diving team would have its own dedicated chase boat to ensure against the worse case scenario that has all the teams separated from the wreck and drifting at sea.

Regardless of the environment, teams should have a plan that accounts for the following contingencies:

1. Diver separated from surface support or fails to appear at the prearranged time
   a. Search procedure
   b. Notes indicating time, depth, current, etc., taken for rescue personnel
2. Injured diver in need of medical care and transportation
   a. Proper contact information
   b. Most efficient transportation (i.e., land, sea, air)
3. Proper procedure for managing decompression sickness and/or other injuries
   a. First aid for DCS or injury
   b. Recompression when no other viable options exist
4. Procedure for injured diver while other divers are still in the water
   a. Do not strand other teams
   b. Transportation for injured diver
5. Procedure for managing sudden change in diving conditions (most notably bad weather/currents)
6. Procedure for managing the damage or loss of support vessel

Gas diver and GUE Research Director Todd Kincaid takes a shift on surface support during the Britannic 99 project.

©GUE, Kea, Greece

©Jarrod Jablonski

Divers must always know how to contact the local Emergency Medical System and have the means to do so, such as a cell phone.

Chapter 10

Rescue Diving

Rescue diving techniques are commonly ignored or de-emphasized in open water diving classes. Typically, these classes are conducted in very short time periods, which arguably give them insufficient time to emphasize even basic diving techniques. Therefore, many educators feel that open water divers are incapable of learning any additional skills, while others prefer not to even discuss the possibility of getting hurt while diving. Not participating in rescue training is a convenient way to shorten diver training, but is arguably not in the best interest of individual divers. This is because, generally, divers who do not possess fundamental rescue techniques are unlikely to be good divers.

The Non-Rescue

Divers that lack basic rescue skills are not only less capable of assisting a troubled diver, they are also less in tune with what will trigger such a situation. Knowing how to manage a crisis usually entails that one knows what precipitated it, and prepares one to be able to prevent it. Foregoing basic discussions of rescue and assistance does not only not provide divers with the information they need to safely assist divers in distress, it also puts them at a disadvantage with regard to their own safety.

Most emergency situations are the culmination of several poorly managed situations. For example, a diver who runs out of air at depth makes a series of errors before the onset of his/her crisis. First, s/he needed better gas planning for that time and depth. Secondly, s/he should have monitored his/her gauge carefully and not let his/her gas supply vanish without noticing it. Third, s/he should have been close enough to a dive buddy to be easily assisted. These considerations reflect several ways a diver can protect him/herself, and speak to the best form of rescue, namely, self-rescue, where a diver preempts problems by being aware of them.

Though self-rescue is a critical skill to have, it is also vital to acknowledge the important ways in which an astute dive buddy is an asset. A good dive buddy is able to request sensible dive and gas planning, can monitor levels of stress and breathing rate, can be aware of a depleting breathing supply, and can be quick to notice a diver that is out of air. Astute dive buddies that are aware, and that are encouraged to provide assistance, often circumvent problems before they occur. Operating together, divers can eliminate all but the most unusual and catastrophic emergencies. In other words, they can remove nearly all the risk attached to diving.

Things to be aware of while diving, in both oneself and in one's team members, are signs of stress. These include:

1. Rapid or shallow breathing
2. Rapid or unusual body movements
3. Wide-eyed look of fear or concern
4. Struggling at depth or at the surface[1]
5. Divers that appear to be ready or in the process of a panicked flight to the surface
6. Abandonment of any life support equipment such as a mouthpiece or mask
7. Unusually clumsy behavior
8. Lack of response to signals or communication
9. Unusually poor trim or buoyancy control

A flotation device such as a diver's life raft or even a buoyancy compensator will be invaluable when assisting an exhausted diver.

[1] It is important to note that, on the surface, divers in distress rarely call out or signal for assistance.

Assisting Tired Divers

Exhausted divers can be helped using several different towing methods; these include the arm-in-arm, the fin push, and the tank pull. The arm-in-arm tow allows rescuers to get close to the diver, and can calm a stressed diver while providing, if necessary, good body position for rescue breathing. The fin push is often the most efficient propulsion technique, as it allows individuals to swim with a horizontal posture while using a powerful flutter kick, but is lacking in that it makes talking to the distressed diver difficult (which often reduces stress). The tank tow allows a reasonably efficient towing, with moderate communication ability.

Rescue Diving Skills

All divers should be properly trained in CPR and First Aid, and should enroll in a diver rescue class. Properly prepared divers are far more likely to be able to safely manage unusually stressful situations than unprepared ones. However, actual "rescues" should be a last resort, and if they take place, usually indicate a failure to manage minor problems and/or a lack of attention to signs of stress. Divers that properly monitor themselves, and their dive buddies, for signs of escalating stress are nearly always able to avoid rescue techniques.

In the event that divers are unable to prevent a situation from deteriorating into a rescue, they should note several important guidelines. First, divers who are experiencing a great deal of stress typically require prompt assistance. Escalating stress will often result in panic, which is far more difficult to manage. Second, divers who are running low on, or

Those divers who receive proper dive rescue training will be far more likely to effectively manage diving emergencies.

©Jarrod Jablonski

are out of, breathing gas will usually calm down quickly when given additional breathing supplies. Lastly, stressed divers are often calmed by the close presence of another diver, and will respond positively to both eye-to-eye and physical contact.

Panicked Divers

When stress levels climb out of control, they lead a diver into panic. In a panic-stricken state, individuals are unable to think rationally; fear takes control. Most panic-stricken divers try to grab others and/or bolt for the surface. Irrational ascents to the surface are very dangerous in all situations, particularly in overhead environments, or in situations where one is subject to a decompression obligation. If stress becomes a problem, divers should stop and focus on slow, deep breathing, taking time to bring down the escalating levels of stress.

Divers that are panicking can be not only difficult to manage, but also dangerous; they can potentially compromise a rescue diver's safety in a variety of ways, the most obvious being when a rescue diver is grabbed and unwillingly submerged by the panicked diver. Divers are unlikely to be able to break free from the grip of a panicked diver, and in the wrong situation may find themselves at great peril. Therefore, when dealing with a panicked diver, rescuers should avoid contact whenever possible. This can be done in several ways. If a panicked diver is on the surface, then the most important thing is to help him/her establish neutral buoyancy. One can do this without contact by prompting him/her to drop their weight belt and/or by supplying him/her with additional floatation; the latter can take the form of a buoyancy compensator, floatation ring, cushion or other buoyant item. Floatation devices will greatly simplify a rescuer's ability to manage a panicked diver. Should the rescuer be unable to provide additional floatation, and/or is not able to get the panicked diver buoyant, they may need to drop the diver's weight belt by going underwater and reaching up to release the belt. Alternatively, rescuers may be able to inflate the diver's BC. It is preferable to do this from behind the diver to prevent oneself from being grabbed. Remember, a distressed diver on the surface is primarily in need of buoyancy, and is likely too stressed to realize how easily they could solve their own problem. In most cases, even minor assistance or direction is sufficient.

Approaching Divers On the Surface

In some cases, a stressed diver will surface in sight of individuals who are on shore or in a boat. This situation will require an individual to swim out to the diver and provide him/her with assistance. Rescuers wearing fins and a mask are much more efficient at swimming to a distant diver than those without them. Where possible, divers should bring fins and buoyancy. Ideally, other divers would follow these rescuers, wearing SCUBA, should the initial rescuers be unable to reach the victim in time. When longer distances must be traversed, or sea conditions prohibit proper sighting, the rescuer should be guided by a surface spotter.

Unconscious Divers

As with most life-threatening situations, the proper management of an unconscious diver depends on a speedy response, good choices, and luck. Numerous remarkable stories pay tribute to the successful rescue of an unconscious diver. In cold water (less than 70° F/20° C), divers have been revived after as long as 70 minutes of immersion. Though the resuscitation of victims after long immersions is more the exception than the rule, it is, nonetheless, a testament to the possibilities inherent in an emergency situation.[2]

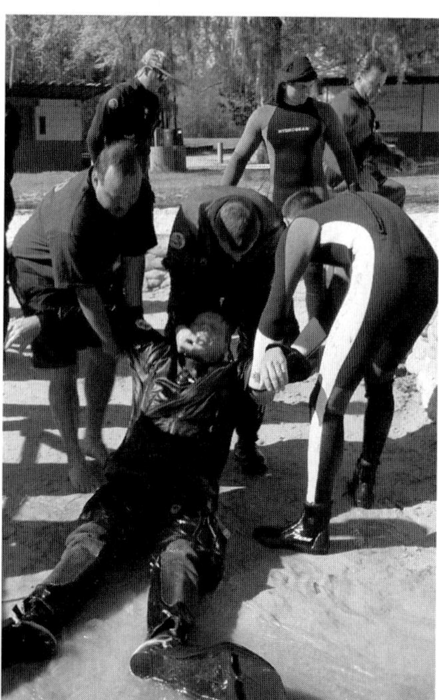

©David Rhea, Jackson Blue, Florida

Care must be given to stabilize the unconscious diver at every stage from in-water to the surface.

[2] Cf., <u>Ventilation Basics,</u> later on in this chapter, gives a more robust treatment of these issues.

Unconscious Diver At the Surface

An unconscious diver at the surface should be stabilized with their mouth out of the water. This is generally done by floating the diver on their back and by stabilizing the head. Following this, an airway should be established, and breathing, pulse, and general conditions verified. If a boat is available, it is preferable that the boat comes to the victim and rescuer. If it is necessary for the rescuer to swim to the shore or to the support vessel, great care should be taken to ensure that the victim's airway is maintained and that water is kept from entering the mouth. Some individuals prefer to use mouth to nose breathing for in-water resuscitation. Divers must assess their ability to keep water out of the airway in this and, in fact, all water rescue techniques.

If the victim is not breathing, then the rescuer must breathe for the victim (CPR is not feasible in the water). If the victim is without a pulse, the rescuer should breathe for the victim, and make haste for an area where CPR is possible. Breathing is commonly done mouth-to-mouth by pinching the nose, or by holding the mouth shut and breathing mouth-to-nose. Breathing cycles should conform to commonly accepted ventilation standards. If surface conditions are favorable (very little wave action), then it is better to remove the victim's mask and ensure a good mouth-to-mouth seal and a proper nose pinch. In higher seas, it may be better to keep the victim's mask on to protect the airway.

Breathing for the victim could also take the form of positive pressure from a SCUBA regulator.[3] Air delivered from a scuba regulator may (in

Recent studies indicate that regulator-assisted ventilation is a powerful tool for the CPR-trained rescue diver.

©David Rhea, Jackson Blue, Florida

[3] Cf., Ventilation basics and regulator use later on in this section.

the case of Nitrox) deliver a noticeably higher percentage of oxygen to the victim. Furthermore, in rough surface conditions, using a regulator to deliver gas to a victim can help to protect the airway, and to limit the risk of introducing water into the breathing passage. However, one must be aware that the excess air delivered via the regulator could create a lung expansion injury.

Unconscious Diver At Depth

An unconscious diver at depth calls for a particularly speedy response on the part of the rescuer. Established wisdom recommends leaving the victim's regulator where it was found. For example, if the regulator is out of the victim's mouth when s/he is found, the traditional recommendation is that it is left like that. This is because, if an unconscious diver loses the regulator from their mouth, chances are that the airway will be filled with water. Rescuers should recognize that the only definitive treatment here is to bring the diver to the surface, and should make every effort to do so, unless decompression or overhead restrictions prohibit this. In any event, the rescuer should first get a firm hold on the victim, by running the right hand under the victim's right shoulder, and holding the regulator in the mouth by placing pressure on the chin. The rescuer can then use the left hand to control buoyancy, dumping air as necessary (it is best to operate the victim's B.C., after venting one's own, to prevent a runaway ascent from expanding air). Anyhow, the rescuer should prioritize getting the victim to the surface under a controlled ascent. Upon reaching the surface, the rescuer should treat the victim as an unconscious victim described above.

In the event that it is not feasible (i.e., overhead or decompression) to take the victim directly to the surface, the rescuer must evaluate several options. If the victim and rescuer are both under a significant decompression obligation, the rescuer must decide where the risk is highest. If surface support is available, it is generally best to deliver the victim to surface support, and return to decompression. After doing so, the rescuer should quickly return to decompression (three minutes or less), because the risk of DCS to the rescuer greatly increases with time spent at the surface. In this scenario, although the victim and possibly the rescuer may suffer DCS, DCS is treatable; death by drowning is not.

Should the decompression obligation be significant, or overhead conditions prohibit bringing the victim to the surface, the rescuer has little choice but to attempt in-water regulator ventilation. The effectiveness of such rescue is unknown. Heroic efforts are not likely to succeed; but, nonetheless, they provide the victim with some chance of survival.

By ventilating the victim with a SCUBA regulator (see below), there is some chance, however small, that s/he may return to consciousness and be able to undergo proper decompression. Again the ultimate goal would be to safely remove them from the overhead, while at the same time preventing significant amounts of water from entering their lungs; one way to do this would be to invert them (head down) and vent the water from their breathing passage.

In many cases, unconscious divers can be brought to the surface. When this is the case, it is best to bring an unconscious diver to the surface.

Reasons for Losing Consciousness

Divers may lose consciousness under water for a variety of reasons; these include:

Hypoxia or CO poisoning: If this were suspected, using the victim's breathing gas at any point in the rescue would be unwise. Rescuers should use only a known breathable source.

Seizure: In some cases, seizures are "survivable." Transient apnea is common after a seizure, but usually lasts only seconds or a minute or two. In an air environment, death from an oxygen seizure is extremely unlikely. However, in an underwater environment, a seizure would require that the airway of the victim be protected and maintained, and s/he be possibly ventilated for a short period of time. Again, the use of an alternate gas mix to ventilate the victim may be beneficial. An additional consid-

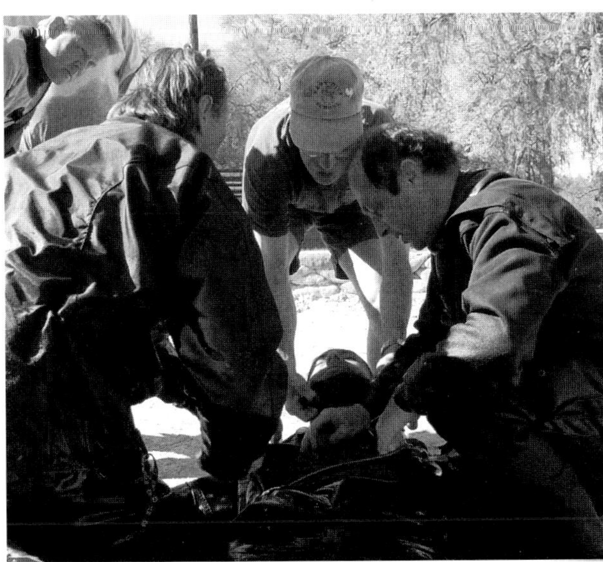

WKPP dive team members practice preparing an unconscious diver for oxygen ventilation.

©David Rhea, Jackson Blue, Florida

eration here is that, when divers awaken from an oxygen seizure, they will not be cooperative, but very disoriented and most likely extremely difficult to manage.

Narcosis: Historically, this is associated with a breathing but "unresponsive" diver. Maintaining an airway and ascending to shallower depth may restore cognition. However, the most sensible alternative here is to avoid narcosis all together by using only responsible gas mixes.

Out-of-gas drowning: It is likely difficult to resuscitate a victim in this category; however, if there is time, and no other reasonable options, ventilation attempts are worthwhile.

Ventilating an Apneic Victim with a SCUBA Regulator

The process discussed below is experimental, and has only been tested on a very small population. This discussion should not be mistaken for common practice, but as an outline of a logical procedure to be taken in an otherwise hopeless situation.

Ventilation Basics

In a non-breathing patient, one's primary objective should be to establish 100% oxygen ventilation; one's secondary objective should be to eliminate carbon dioxide. Though the elimination of carbon dioxide is important here, it is not as important as it is to maintain proper oxygen levels in the organism; this is because brain cells die rapidly without oxygen. Therefore, in a situation where there is compromised ventilation or circulation, the higher levels of oxygen delivered, the better. In an otherwise healthy individual, once ventilation and oxygenation are established, re-establishing circulation is usually easy. Initial response, "bystander" CPR has traditionally employed mouth-to-mouth resuscitation for rescue, which delivers 17 percent oxygen to the patient. While far better than not breathing at all, mouth-to-mouth resuscitation delivers a relatively low concentration of oxygen. This is especially true when pulmonary exchange of gases has been compromised, as in the case of near drowning. In a non-breathing patient, the ideal method of resuscitation is endo-tracheal intubation and 100 percent oxygen ventilation. This requires training and experience, and may be impractical in some emergency situations. Mask ventilation, using 100 percent oxygen, is a second alternative, but also requires training and experience. Even if ventilation is less than perfect, adequate oxygen may be delivered if the oxygen concentration is high.

VENTILATION COMPLICATIONS

Manual ventilation can cause serious complications in victims, even in highly trained hands. *Gastric insufflation*, or forcing air into the stomach, is the most common, and is primarily caused by high ventilation pressure with inadequate opening of the airway. Gastric insufflation is more of a problem in individuals who suffer from obesity, non-compliant lungs (e.g., smoking) or airway abnormalities. Gastric insufflation increases the chance of vomiting, and of aspirating the gastric contents, which can prove fatal.

Manual ventilation can also lead to lung over-pressurization and to several types of barotrauma, including *pneumothorax* (collapsed lung), *mediastinal emphysema* (gas surrounding the heart) and *subcutaneous emphysema* (gas under the skin). To prevent these problems, Advanced Cardiac Life Support programs suggest maximum inspiratory rates of 40 liters/minute and maximum pressures of 60 centimeters of H_2O in any mechanical ventilation device. While flow rates of SCUBA regulators are far above 40 liters/minute, due to the exhaust valve, the maximum pressures are well below 60 centimeters of H_2O.

In the end, the ultimate complication from ventilation is failure to ventilate, which is always deadly. Avoiding the complications of ventilation is desirable, but should not prevent one from attempting to treat someone who will die if not treated.

TECHNIQUES

The ideal situation would be intubation or a bag mask system with 100 percent oxygen. Oxygen-supplied power mask inflators are available, but not widely used by the non-medical field because they can easily lead to over pressurization injuries like pneumothorax. All divers have regulators and, hopefully, a range of gases at their disposal, from air to 100% oxygen. Of course, in the apneic victim, the higher the oxygen levels are during the ventilation, the better. The American Heart Association Advance Cardiac Life Support guidelines suggest tidal volumes of 10-15 ml/kg, which typically would be about 700-1000cc in the average fit person. Since resting tidal volumes are around 500 milliliters, CPR does not require excessive volumes to supply adequate ventilation. Using a non-rebreathing SCUBA regulator is not ideal, but may suffice until proper equipment becomes available.

A SCUBA regulator is gas-powered, and, with some practice, can be operated with one hand. SCUBA regulators are reported to deliver well over the suggested rate of flow for powered ventilation; furthermore, the extremely low cracking pressure of a regulator's exhalation valve makes over-inflation of the lungs unlikely in comparison to manual ventilation systems. Using it to ventilate, one would use one hand for the regulator and the other to close the nose. The regulator would be placed in the mouth, as it would be in a conscious person, and the little and ring fingers placed below the body of the mandible to hold the airway open by lifting the jaw. Thumb and middle finger hold the regulator in place, while the index finger intermittently presses the purge valve to inflate the lungs. The purge is virtually an on or off valve. It is depressed until the chest rises; in most people this would take two to three seconds, but could be longer. When using a bag-, mask-, or valve-type system, the inhalation time is less, because, without leaking, these methods generate more pressure. With the open exhaust valve in the second stage, it takes longer to give a breath, because not all of the gas is going into the lungs. The amount of time that the purge valve is held down is based on how long it takes for the chest to rise.

Visual verification of lung expansion is important in gauging amount and timing of inspiration. Listening for and feeling the expiration of gas from the lung confirms ventilation, although air in the stomach can mimic breathing in an unconscious person. Between administered breaths, the victim should be allowed to fully exhale. Too rapid ventilation and inadequate exhalation can cause gas trapping in the lungs, and can lead to over-pressurization injuries. In these procedures, large volumes of gas are wasted because the regulator exhalation valve is forced open when the purge valve is pressed. Timing is similar to conventional CPR.

Clinical experience

There is no scientific study available to verify the effectiveness of this technique. GUE representatives have ventilated an apneic, anaesthetized patient using a Scuba Pro Mk10/ G250 with air. Air was chosen so that inadequate ventilation could be quickly detected using continuous pulse oximetry. Oxygen saturations could be maintained above 98 percent using air, indicating adequate ventilation.

Complications

This technique should not be attempted by someone without CPR experience or without an understanding of how to maintain an airway. These techniques are not intended for introductory divers, but rather intended for experienced divers with lifesaver training. A corollary here is that divers involved in more advanced diving should have at least basic life support training. Most criticisms of this technique fall into several categories.

Too difficult. This may be true under some circumstances, but practice will develop skills for use in rescue circumstances.

Water leaks into the airway without a good fit. This is true only if the head is submerged, which is the number one lesson in basic rescue courses.

Too much pressure or gas flow. This would not to be a problem with most regulators because of the exhaust valve, which limits the ability to develop positive pressure.

Too little inflation pressure. This is probably the biggest weakness with regulator ventilation. It is very possible in a large person with non-compliant lungs and/or constricting gear that a regulator might not be able to generate enough pressure to adequately ventilate him/her.

Legal issues. The legality of choosing this method likely falls under the Good Samaritan clause. Please refer to legal advice and the disclaimer at the start of this section.

Do no harm. It is preferable to have a live diver with a treatable injury (pneumo-thorax), than a dead diver without one. Successful outcome in resuscitation is determined largely by the delay of treatment. Seek training in airway management as well as CPR. It will always be a matter of personal judgment how aggressive one should be in their attempt to rescue an injured diver. Nonetheless, always remember not to harm yourself or others in futile rescue attempts.

The previous discussion is not based on scientific studies, and is not to be taken as the proper standard of care for all cases. It is simply an educated belief, one based on logical analysis of likely circumstances; it still lacks adequate proof and field confirmation. The techniques advanced there are additional tools for an emergency. If you do not understand them, feel untrained to use them, or cannot master them, please use what you know best. Like any other technique, if regulator ventilation fails to ventilate the victim, promptly do something else.[4]

[4] For a more thorough treatment of regulator ventiliation consult GUE's Technical Diving Manual.

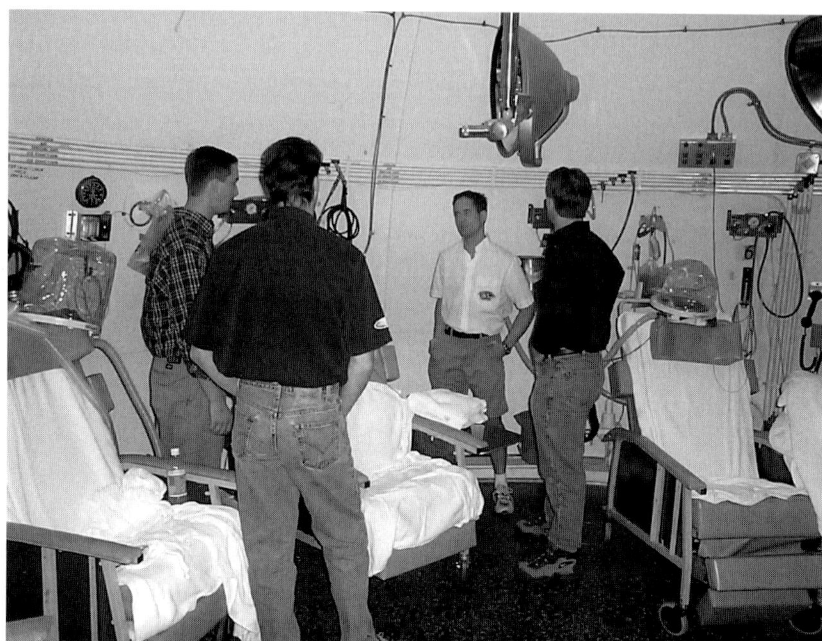

Lower left ©David Rhea; all other photos ©GUE

Top: The Duke Center for Hyperbaric Medicine's primary hyperbaric operating chamber; Lower right: A surface tender watches over the communications hardware during a recovery in a water filled sump in the mountains above Los Angeles; Lower left: GUE instructor Tyler Moon debriefs a student following a Cave 2 training dive in North Florida.

CHAPTER 11

ACCIDENT ANALYSIS: ARE YOU AT RISK?

Few SCUBA diving courses include a discussion of diving accidents. In fact, many open water classes strive to avoid any mention of serious risk or death. Though it is unlikely, one could attribute this reticence to the fact that, realistically, fatalities are quite unusual in SCUBA diving; there are roughly only four deaths per 100,000 divers (B&E p 240). Nonetheless, there is good reason to discuss diving accidents during a SCUBA course because, by discussing accidents and the factors that contribute to them, divers can become more cognizant of what will expose them to risk and what will not.

©Jarrod Jablonski

Divers who are proficient in open water diving, even instructors, are ill-prepared to deal with the dangers of an overhead environment without formal training.

Cave diver training was shaped by the community's experience with the primary causes of fatalities in caves. A brief overview of cave diver accident analysis is always helpful, in that it helps one to understand the benefits of accident review. Cave diving accident analysis is generally split between risks associated with the average (not cave-certified) diver entering a cave, and risks associated with the trained cave diver entering

Elliott, D. H. and Bennett, P. B. "Underwater Accidents." The Physiology and Medicine of Diving. 4th Ed., pp. 238-252. Ed. P. Bennett & D. Elliott. London: W. B. Saunders Co. Ltd. 1993 a cave; it established that there were five primary safety violations that accounted for nearly all cave diving fatalities.

1. Lack of cave training
2. Lack of continuous guideline
3. Failure to reserve two thirds of gas supply for exit
4. Diving to excess depth
5. Diving without sufficient lighting (i.e., at least one primary and two reserve lights)

When these categories were first articulated in the 1980's they provided a reasonably accurate measure of what usually went wrong on a fatal cave dive. Although they are still good at establishing primary risk factors, today these standards are less complete, serving to create the illusion of well-defined risk.[1] Nonetheless, what is important for our purposes is to recognize the value of accident analysis for training purposes.

How Do Cave Fatalities Relate To Recreational Diving?

The preceding section focused on cave diving risk factors because, despite their limitations, they serve to highlight problems that are relevant to all forms of diving. By modifying these, we can begin to articulate certain principles that will limit recreational diver risk.

[1] Whatever the degree of statistical precision associated with this early analysis, it is nonetheless distorted by a number of factors, including the changing diving popularity, advances in technology, and effectiveness in the education of risk factors. In other words, the early, and careful, accumulation of statistics measuring cave diving fatalities was very instructive, while later review becomes less relevant, particularly to certified cave divers. For example, consider the following standard violations: diving to excess depth, diving without a continuous guideline, and diving without sufficient gas reserves. These illustrate cave diving's early risk factors, as they were understood at the time; however, limited review of these factors calls into question their present accuracy. For example, diving to excess depth is undoubtedly a risk factor, but a review of fatalities associated with the violation of this standard suggests that the most likely reason for the majority of these fatalities is diving on air at depth and its resultant narcotic impairment. Information of this sort is essential to proper planning and safe diving activity.

The following discussion outlines a set of errors that can be directly associated with diving accidents. These are:

- Exceeding one's level of training
- Going beyond one's personal level of comfort and/or ability
- Diving beyond the range of one's gas mixture
- Using improper or insufficient equipment

Exceeding One's Level of Training

Environmental factors (e.g., temperature, current, and overheads) contribute to 62% of all recreational diving fatalities (DSM pp. 439). Individuals that are proficient in one area of diving are very often ill prepared for the dangers of another. One of the most valuable aspects to diver training is helping individuals properly identify and manage the risks associated with a type of diving that they are interested in pursuing, but for which they lack training. Proper training does not insulate one against risk, but it can help to outline areas of particular concern, and to prepare individuals by helping them cultivate proper techniques and sensible diving practices.

Going Beyond One's Personal Level of Comfort

Training is a central component to diving safety; but without common sense and honest personal evaluation, it can be nearly meaningless. Far too many divers view a certification card as insurance against risk. In truth, certification cards are largely a license to begin learning beyond the guidance of an instructor. During proper training, divers should gain an appreciation for the risk and management of common problems, and an understanding of personal ability and fitness. For example, 25% of recreational fatalities involve divers that were not medically fit to dive (DSM pp. 439).

The burden of evaluating personal ability and fitness ultimately falls on the individual diver. Divers must be sensible about the risks of a particular dive, choosing not to partake in one that exceeds their zone of comfort and ability. Proper training is responsible for providing the diver with an understanding of the objective risks associated with a given activity; it is the responsibility of the certified diver to utilize this information to make their own decision regarding that activity.

Diving Beyond the Range of One's Gas Mixture

Technical divers regularly lose their lives breathing inappropriate mixtures. In all but the most careless situations, this type of accident is uncommon among recreational divers. Nonetheless, all divers should always be on guard against using improper breathing mixtures. Most improper gas usage involves technical divers accidentally breathing the wrong decompression mixture at depth (i.e., accidentally breathing oxygen instead of Nitrox). These errors nearly always seem to relate to poor tank marking and to poor gas switching procedures.[2] Furthermore, diving gases that exceed 1.4 PO_2 (except during decompression), and 100 foot END, threaten diver safety and should not be used. In the case of recreational divers, they merely need to ensure that their breathing mixture maintains an oxygen content with a PO_2 below 1.4. This is most easily accomplished by diving GUE's standard 32% mixture on dives that are shallower than 100' (30m).

Using Improper or Insufficient Equipment

The most obvious case of using improper equipment involves individuals diving in an environment without the necessary safety equipment. Examples include: divers entering an overhead without a guideline, ice divers not using a surface line, divers drifting without a surface marker, deep divers using substandard regulators, and divers entering a cave without sufficient lighting. Countless fatalities point to the need for

For an inexperienced diver, dealing with multiple bottles can be a source of stress.

©Barry Miller/GUE

[2] Technical Divers can consult the GUE Technical Diving Manual for information on handling multiple breathing mixtures.

proper equipment; divers that ignore this place themselves at much greater risk. Diving is not the type of activity that allows equipment to be safely cobbled together from odd pieces.

Stress on the Diver

No discussion of accident analysis would be complete without addressing the role of stress in accidents and fatalities. By stress, we are referring to factors that evoke a physical and often psychological response. Many activities result in an accumulation of stress, and its presence often performs a valuable service by alerting us to an approaching threat. One's goal is not to eliminate all forms of stress, but to maintain control over them, and to recognize their message. Realistically, many fatalities result from fairly simple mistakes that are improperly managed. These can accumulate and overwhelm the diver.

Consider, for example, a diver that is improperly weighted and that suffers from poor trim and/or buoyancy. This diver is likely over exerting and, with increasing stress levels, accumulating CO_2. Should the diver or one of his/her team members note this problem, then the team could be notified, the problem rectified and/or the dive terminated. If not, then the diver can be (and has been) pushed to go beyond his/her comfort level, both psychologically and physiologically, and then on into panic and death.

Recognizing Stress

The initial stages of stress often evoke minor changes. An individual may begin to breathe more rapidly and may find it difficult to remain cognizant of their surroundings. Additionally, stressed divers often experience perceptual narrowing and increased clumsiness. Elevated breathing rates are often accompanied by shallow breathing, which does not properly vent the lungs and which leads to carbon dioxide retention. CO_2 retention can itself lead to higher levels of stress, as excess levels of carbon dioxide stimulate a respiratory response that creates a feeling of urgency. As the diver attempts to replenish the needed oxygen, the result is often rapid, shallow breathing. This poor lung ventilation can lead to even higher levels of carbon dioxide in the bloodstream, and to higher stress levels in a dangerous feedback cycle. While experiencing stress, a diver should stop, breathe slowly and deeply for several cycles, and then evaluate the situation. Often, all that is required is time to catch one's breath; but it is important not to let stress get beyond one's control.

When a diver feels that their stress levels are mounting, they should stop and breathe deeply, venting the lungs of excess carbon dioxide and introducing much needed oxygen. While rapid, uncontrolled breathing is a common reaction to stress, other relatively obvious signs may also present themselves. Divers who find it difficult to remain aware of their surroundings are frequently said to be experiencing tunnel vision. These divers focus on one particular object to the exclusion of their surroundings. This lack of attention may result in any number of negative consequences, i.e., lost line, lost dive buddy, violation of proper air rules and poor fin technique. Most divers become clumsy in the presence of stress. A clumsy individual is more likely to become entangled in the line or crash to the floor, perhaps disturbing the sediments. Divers who experience reduced control are likely to hit obstructions, damaging the environment, their equipment and themselves.

Coping with Stress

The best way to manage stress is to remain alert and anticipate its development. One should not force oneself into overtly stressful situations.

© Wes Sadler

Rapid breathing, lack of attention to surroundings and/or clumsy behavior of a dive buddy may be the first signs of stress. The DIR dive team should be aware of the comfort level of each member and maintain constant communication among team members throughout the dive.

Instead, high levels of stress indicate the need for the team to stop and regain focus. Do not be afraid to stop or force an errant buddy to stop and gain control. Many fatalities are the sequential combination of several poorly managed problems, as individuals frequently make poor decisions in stressful situations. By increasing one's fitness level and by remaining committed to halting dives that burgeon out of control, divers will be able to regain control of their stress and manage the situation effectively. Each diver is responsible not only for monitoring their stress levels, but also for remaining aware of signs that other team members are not comfortable.

Panic

When stress levels climb out of control, they lead a diver into panic. In a panic-stricken state, individuals are unable to think rationally, and fear takes control. Most panic-stricken divers try to grasp others and/or bolt for the surface. Irrational ascents to the surface are very dangerous at any time, but particularly in an overhead environment or when one has a decompression obligation. If stress becomes a problem, divers should stop and focus on slow, deep breathing, taking time to bring down the escalating levels of stress.

Stress levels can be controlled with relative ease, and most divers find that a few dives into a new environment are all that are needed to increase their comfort level. If a diver feels inordinately stressed while diving, they should terminate the dive and evaluate their diving activities. The world is replete with exciting and fascinating activities. If diving in general or a particular kind of diving is not fun for an individual, then it should be forsaken for other activities regardless of desire or peer pressure. Heavy stress eliminates what should be an enjoyable activity, while uncontrolled stress results in panic, which is rarely survivable.

©Steve Auer, Wakulla Springs State Park, Florida

DIR techniques provide the foundation for a lifetime of dive adventures.

Conclusion

Doing it Right

Divers are ultimately responsible for their own decisions, and are expected to make reasonable choices with respect to diving environments and individual dive plans. However, individuals with proper training and with a clear picture of common diving mistakes will be more prepared to make good choices. One of the most common problems plaguing divers today is the inability to properly evaluate personal ability and/or environmental risk. Without this ability, divers cannot make informed judgments. Unfortunately, weakness in this area is directly traceable to abbreviated training and to a poor emphasis on personal fitness and responsibility.

Divers who lack the basic diving skills and fitness levels discussed in the preceding sections should reconsider whether they are prepared to dive. Because the risk of diving ultimately falls on the individual (and their team), divers must strive to honestly evaluate their abilities and their degree of comfort in the water. Being certified should never be taken as a guarantee of ability. The combination of subjective assessment, varying dedication to basic skill development, and differences in instructional proficiency creates a wide range of skills in similarly certified divers.

In the last couple of decades, diving has become progressively identified as an activity that anyone can pursue. While the majority of individuals are capable of SCUBA diving, the majority are not willing to develop the skill proficiency and fitness required to safely pursue diving; nonetheless, they do, encouraged by a financially motivated industry. It is important to note, however, that weakness in diving skills and lack of fitness generally reduces the level of fun and enjoyment that can be derived from diving. Furthermore, these weaknesses can also place the individual and his/her team diving at greater risk than they need to be. Certainly, very simple dives in warm, shallow environments require limited proficiency, but poorly practiced divers have found themselves in trouble even in the simplest of environments

There are many interesting activities, other than diving, that one can engage in; and individuals who are not keen in investing a minimal amount of effort to developing sound basic diving skills, to improving streamlining and fitness, would be better served by taking up one of these. However, individuals that are willing to make this investment can reap huge rewards in diving fun and enjoyment.

It is increasingly common for diving educators to emphasize the ease of diving, pretending that no real investment in time or effort is necessary. This reduced emphasis on skill and fitness fosters the idea that these aspects are superfluous. Yet, diving is very much like life, in that you get out of it what you invest in it. Individuals interested in maximizing their fun and enjoyment will find that simple actions produce surprising returns. These investments are similar to financial investments, in that the interest they bear is usually compounded. Small changes and minimal effort result in substantial rewards.

Diving is indeed one of the world's most enjoyable activities. However, the stress and discomfort associated with unrefined skills are often thought to be a common part of the diving experience. This is the area in which divers are led astray, often by well-meaning educators emphasizing the fun of diving. Unnecessary obstacles will always limit divers that are unwilling to invest in proper diving techniques. On the other hand, divers who are willing to invest in their diving, who are willing to embrace and conform to sound diving principles, to fitness, training, and good skills, are well on their way to experiencing great enjoyment in the underwater realm. They will be doing it right.

For more information about Global Underwater Explorers or about Doing It Right Diving, please visit www.gue.com.

Index

A

B

I

J

K

L

M

N

O

P

T